GRADUATES INTO INDUSTRY

for April

Graduates into Industry

A Survey of Changing Graduate Attitudes

CHRISTOPHER MABEY
Henley, The Management College

Gower

Published by
Gower Publishing Company Limited
Gower House
Croft Road
Aldershot
Hants GU11 3HR
England

Gower Publishing Company
Old Post Road
Brookfield
Vermont 05036
USA

British Library Cataloguing in Publication Data
Mabey, Christopher
  Graduates into industry
  1. College graduates——Employment——Great
  Britain
  I. Title
  331.11'423   HD6278.G7

ISBN 0-566-00886-6

Printed in Great Britain by Blackmore Press, Shaftesbury, Dorset

Contents

List of tables

List of figures

Acknowledgements

My thanks are due to a number of staff at Henley, the Management College where this research was conceived and conducted from, and in particular to Professor David Birchall who offered encouragement, critical advice and help in securing company access.

I would also like to thank the representatives of the 20 companies who cooperated in this project and each of their respective graduate entrants who responded to the questionnaires.

1 The mismatch

Between 1981-82 three separate and significant reports were published in this country which highlighted a problem of alarming proportions with serious economic, organizational and social consequences.

Beginning in 1977 the Department of Employment's Unit for Manpower Studies launched a national survey of those who had graduated from UK universities and polytechnics in 1970 (Williamson 1981). Information concerning the selection and entry of occupations, descriptions of employers and flows between sectors were gathered from over 12,000 graduates, representing approximately one in five of the 1970 cohort. Simultaneously a similar study, concentrating more on inter-sector mobility - was conducted by the Institute of Manpower Studies amongst 264 graduate employers and 1,300 graduates who had left these companies during 1979-80 (Parsons and Hutt 1981; Hutt and Parsons 1981). A number of important findings emerged from these two complementary and extensive surveys:-

(1) The voluntary turnover of graduate entrants from their first employer is high: '70 per cent of the graduates were still with the employer who had recruited them after two years, and 52 per cent after five years'. (Hutt and Parsons 1981, p 29). This retention rate was particularly poor for those companies in the 'engineering and allied industries' sector, where only 44 per cent of the original graduate intake remained with the company five years later.

(2)   Widespread disenchantment was found among graduate
leavers: 'graduates   changed   jobs   because   they   were
dissatisfied with the general nature and pace of work,   felt
their abilities were not being fully used,   and saw poor
prospects for career prospects and experience ahead of them'.
(Hutt and Parsons 1981, p 43).   Whereas those men studying
engineering at university were more clearly committed to a
specific   career   in   their   final   years   than   their
contemporaries on other courses, one quarter who subsequently
left their first jobs did so because of dissatisfaction, the
highest proportion to register this reason (Williamson 1981,
pp 4-6).

(3)   When asked about how their jobs matched expectations,
attributes most highly recorded as worse than expected (29-
46%) were management style,   quality of personal supervision
and using their abiities to the full.   About 30 per cent
found the recruitment process in general,   and companies'
representatives specifically,   had given them an inaccurate
picture of their previous job,   and 42 per cent felt that
recruitment literature had misled them.   (Hutt and Parsons
1981, pp 30,31, 43).

In 1977 a Committee of Inquiry into the Engineering
Profession was appointed by the Secretary of State for
Industry to review the manufacturing industry in the light of
national economic needs. (Finniston 1980).   As part of the
data collection for the report, the Committee visited 46 UK
employers, and amongst their comments were the following:-

(1) Companies had difficulties in filling their engineering
vacancies, especially those trained in disciplines specific
to their industry.

(2)   Manufacturing organizations voiced difficulties in
attracting graduates to work in production, and a general
criticism of many new graduates 'was their lack of
appreciation of industrial and business "nous" in that they
did not recognise the importance of marketing and supplying
customer needs and had little understanding of the economics
of production'. (Finniston 1980, pp 194-195).

(3) Perhaps related to the above points, the sandwich course
was widely favoured for producing good practical managers.

The   selected   findings   from   these   independent
sourcesdemonstrate a paradoxical picture of graduate
recruitment and integration. On the one hand there is a high
degree of dissatisfaction amongst graduate recruits -

particularly in the industrial sector - which appears to be linked to inaccurate perceptions fostered during the recruitment process. On the other, manufacturing employers lament the lack of certain types of graduate engineer, and specifically favour those with previous experience of industrial practice.

Clearly, there is a costly and ironical mismatch between graduate resources, potential and aspirations on the one hand and the needs, requirements and opportunities of industrial employers on the other; a mismatch which this study proposes to investigate.

GRADUATE FOLLOW UP STUDIES

In each decade since the 2nd World War a major follow-up survey of graduates has been produced, providing us with a fairly consistent commentary on early turnover. The first was a national, random sample of 6,500 male graduates across arts, science and technology disciplines (P.E.P. 1956). The postal survey showed that during the four years following graduation, a third had left their first employer. Of those graduates originally entering industry and commerce, one in five had moved to another employment sector and, after allowing for counter-balancing inflows from other sectors, there was a net loss from industry and commerce of 11 per cent.

A second major follow-up survey of graduates was conducted in the early 1960's (Kelsall 1970). This time the survey of graduates, begun in 1966, explored the early work experience of over 10,000 students, male and female, who had left UK universities six years previously, and related it to socio-economic background and the career choice process. During this time 28 per cent of male graduates entering industry and 42 per cent of those entering commerce had moved to another employment sector. By contrast, the most stable male group were in education, with a comparable turnover of only 14 per cent since 1960.

Designed deliberately to enable comparison with figures from the Kelsall study was a survey sponsored by the U.M.S. launched in 1977, of 12,000 first degree students who had graduated from universities and polytechnics in 1970 (Williamson 1981). In fact, when again focusing on the numbers leaving their first employment sector, percentages are very similar across the two studies: total outflow, representing graduates 'whose latest job descriptions differ from their first' (Williamson 1979 p 1221) is 27 per cent for university men and 31 per cent for university women. For the industrial sector alone, the respective outflow figures are 27 per cent and 51 per cent.

Helpful as these statistics are in outlining a broad context of inter sector mobility, they nevertheless may disguise the true picture of first job turnover since much of this movement may take place within employment sectors.

Data collected by the I.M.S. (Parsons and Hutt 1981) from 264 employers of graduates in 1981 revealed that after two years 30 per cent of the 1974 cohort had left their first employer, rising to 48 per cent after five years, though there was a considerable variation between firms, regardless of sector. A follow-up study of a selected sample of Reading University applied science graduates seven years after graduation found that one quarter had left their initial employer after only 12 months, and nearly 40 per cent after two years (Atton 1982). A less recent survey of over 1,000 graduates at various times since 1946, showed that only 45 per cent were still with their original employer five years following graduation (B.I.M. 1968).

Thus, to summarise, surveys of both graduates and graduate employers over the years reveal a fairly constant turnover rate of approaching 50 per cent in the first five years' employment; a figure corroborated by another I.M.S. report (Pearson 1976) which spoke of a five year retention rate of little over 60 per cent in most case studies. Furthermore, when analysed by sector, industry and commerce are particularly prone to lose graduate entrants.

Two studies of individual companies, one based at Shell (Hill 1969) and the other at Ford Motor Company (Dunette, Arvey and Banas 1973), shed light of some of the more specific causes of dissatisfaction and turnover amongst graduate entrants. In both cases the attitudes of graduates who had left were compared with those in the same organization who had remained since graduation. Both groups of Shell graduates ranked 27 job features in order of importance and a common profile emerged with intrinsic aspects, like challenge, responsibility, opportunity to learn and use initiative, ranked almost exclusively above extrinsic aspects, such as pay, holiday entitlement, status and working conditions. However when the leaver and the stayer groups ranked the same items according to their satisfaction at Shell, the leavers were considerably less satisfied with virtually all the intrinsic features and withone extrinsic element, namely career and promotion prospects. Dunette et al found a similar disparity between the two groups when dissatisfaction with the most important job features was measured. A crucial variable, the precise length of tenure of the leavers, which in both studies was anything between one and four years, was not measured, however. Also, in the Shell study, respondents were asked to rank order 27 job features; it is doubtful that with so many items to mentally juggle this provides a very accurate measure of prioritised job satisfaction.

A more serious criticism of these and other follow-up studies concerns the validity of asking those who have been working for a company for several years or, even more so, who have since left their employer, to describe retrospectively their satisfactions. Any such evaluation would surely be distorted by their intervening work experience, and not least by the event of leaving itself which has a constraining effect on future attitudes and behaviour (Kiesler 1971). Nevertheless the evidence seems to demonstrate that dissatisfaction with intrinsic job features is a significant phenomenon amongst graduate entrants, and perhaps a central factor in their early departure.

This in turn, suggests that newcomers are seriously misjudging the nature of the job and organization they are joining, and that graduates are perhaps more prone than others to have such unrealistic expectations.

GRADUATE DISENCHANTMENT

A number of descriptive research projects conducted amongst US college graduates show that expectations of employment are consistently inflated. Ward and Athos (1972) collected data on a wide range of job and organization features from MBA prospective employees and matched them with recruiter perceptions of the same companies. The resulting profiles were remarkably similar and, at least from the student perspective, surprisingly positive. Dunette, Arvey and Banas (1973) and Wanous (1976) found that the reality of organizational life was worse than students had anticipated, especially in areas of job satisfaction which they regarded as most important. What is more, this decline in intrinsic expectations continues as students moved from being newcomers to what Wanous calls 'insiders' in the organization. These observations are borne out by a long-term study of graduates entering the American Telegraph and Telephone Company (Bray, Campbell and Grant 1974). Such was the unrealistic optimism of students as they graduated that after seven years working experience, expectations about the job for the remaining

5

sample were still declining — even for the relatively successful managers!

This phenomenon of declining attractiveness has also emerged from studies of the job choice context (Vroom and Deci 1971; Lawler, Kuleck, Rhode and Sorensen 1975), where the initially high estimation of the chosen company, which the authors attribute to post-choice cognitive dissonance, also decreases over time.

It seems that naive expectations are not peculiar to American college graduates. When asked 'How did your image of industry compare with your experience?', 37 per cent of graduates who had been with Shell UK for up to 10 years felt that it had been too favourable; for those who had since left Shell in this period the figure rose to 45 per cent — tenuously suggesting that unmet expectations were a factor in turnover (Hill 1969).

Timperley (1974) compared a cohort of final year Liverpool students with a cohort who had been working in organizations for up to five years. The students group were remarkably more optimistic in their anticipated use of skills and knowledge gained at university than their employed counterparts; though it should be stressed that this was not a longitudinal sample so it is possible that other variables were responsible for the contrast.

How is it then that expectations become so distorted for pre-employment students? Ward and Athos (1972) claim that it is the almost inevitable consequence of students basing their perceptions on the descriptions given by recruiters, who are anxious to portray their companies as positively as possible. Certainly this focus on the recruitment process is an aspect taken up by some of the follow-up surveys. Of 430 Liverpool students in the Easter of their final year, 29 per cent felt that the quantity, and 37 per cent felt that the quality of the careers information that they had received concerning industry and commerce was barely or totally inadequate (Timperley 1974). This was, of course, prior to employment reality so in a sense untested. Atton (1982) canvassed opinions that were well tested, though perhaps too distant for vivid recollection in his study of Reading University graduates seven years later: 22 per cent rated the recruitment process 'not as good as' or 'much worse than expected', and 28 per cent expressed the same opinion of the recruitment literature that they had encountered.

The I.M.S. report on the mobility of young graduates (Parsons

and Hutt 1981) also asked its sample of 1,300 'leaver' graduates about their perceptions of employment information and found a similarly disenchanted view; 34 per cent felt the overall recruitment process had given them a fairly or very inaccurate picture of their previous jobs; 42 per cent found the recruitment literature inaccurate, particularly pronounced in industrial and accountancy sectors, and 31 per cent felt employers' representatives had given an inaccurate picture of previous jobs, though for general management type of work this rose to 45 per cent. Predictably, all three figures reduced dramatically when the same questions were asked about recruitment to present employment: by this time graduates would be far more informed and discerning over career choices. Unfortunately, although these figures are recent and representative of a national population of UK graduates, they are for three reasons limited in their usefulness for the purposes of this research. First, the sampling frame consisted of graduates under 30 years of age who had graduated since 1971. To recall perceptions of prospective employers held in the past is likely to prove unreliable even for the most recent graduates, but especially so for some of the sample who would have left university nearly a decade previously. Second, the sample was comprised of those who had left their employers during 1979; hence, as Parsons and Hutt stress, the results will tend to sound a negative note, since the views of the satisfied 'stayers' are not represented. Finally, over a third of the leavers in this analysis had moved to their previous employer from another job and not direct from higher education. This means that the percentages complaining of pre-job misperceptions are, if anything, an under-estimate since many would have been referring to their second or third job move, by which time the clarity and reality of employment expectations should presumably have improved.

In summary, it has been established by the studies of both US and UK graduates that expectations concerning initial work experience are typically unrealistic; that these first jobs invariably fail to meet the high anticipations of students and inaccurate perceptions engendered by the recruitment process contribute to this mismatch. In many cases, however, findings are based on retrospective judgements and, where detailed, the fulfilment or non-fulfilment of specific expectations are not explored over a period of time.

Wanous' study (1976) is one exception, but his longitudinal data refers to telephone operators rather than students. Furthermore, the link between misleading expectations and subsequent low job satisfaction and turnover is largely assumed rather than explicitly demonstrated (see for instance Dunette et al 1973 p 33;   Parsons and Hutt 1981 p 128-9).

RESEARCH ON SANDWICH COURSES

Although student sandwich courses have been in existence since the beginning of the century, the concept received rapid expansion only in the mid-1950's, being implemented in nine out of ten colleges of Advanced Technology and subsequently as degree courses approved by the CNAA, mainly at polytechnics.   In the decade up to 1979, numbers of sandwich courses doubled to 50,000, comprising 80 per cent men (Pearson 1979).   The most recently reported total is 53,772 (A.S.E.T. 1981); nearly one·half of these are studying engineering and technology, but significant numbers are also pursuing science, social science and business studies (1).

Given the ongoing debate concerning the suitability of graduates (Greenaway and Williams 1973;   Finniston 1980) and postgraduates (Swinnerton-Dyer 1982) for industry's needs, together with the fact that one ninth of the total student population are on sandwich courses, specifically designed for better integration between college and employment, there has been precious little evaluation of sandwich training.   Much has been published describing sandwich education and extolling its virtues to students and industry alike (see Reed, Duncan and Vallance 1980;   Denbury 1976; A.S.E.T 1981), but not usually supported by critical, empirical fieldwork.

Two studies have set about assessing the effectiveness of sandwich courses. Following the establishment of the Diploma in Technology in 1956, Jahoda (1963) undertook an exploratory case study of first year sandwich students taking engineering and science on the diploma course.   The merit of this longitudinal study was its attempt, via three questionnaires over a period of one year, to unravel the process of education using a socio-technical approach (2).   But it was based on 149 students at just one college, and went no further than evaluation of the first industrial training period. There was no comparison with non-sandwich students.

A second more comprehensive analysis was carried out by P.E.P. (Daniel and Pugh 1975). Again it was precipitated by theintroduction of a relatively new course: the CNAA first degree in business studies.   The researchers surveyed 620 graduates from this course who had completed their sandwich courses in 1966 and 1968.   They also received back questionnaires from 91 university business study graduates and 72 CNAA economics graduates - thus enabling a comparison with those non-sandwich graduates on a similar course, and from a similar institution, respectively. They found several interesting differences between these three groups. Compared with their university, non-sandwich counterparts, the CNAA business studies graduates were more likely to find a job earlier, to enter manufacturing industry, to take specific, responsible jobs (as against professional apprenticeships), to work in the full range of managerial functions and initially to achieve higher job levels and earnings - even when the two groups were controlled for age and location. However CNAA business studies graduates were as likely as the other groups to be dissatisfied with their first jobs and more likely to have changed jobs. Further, they had less confidence in the value of their polytechnic qualification, even though it included industrial experience, than did the university graduates in their degrees.

Three findings, relevant to this research, emerge. First, full-time business studies students have greater confidence in their qualifications which would presumably lead to a greater perceived freedom of choice when it comes to job seeking. This is despite facts from the P.E.P. study which indicate that sandwich graduates find jobs more quickly and also enjoy considerably high average earnings. Denbury (1975) cites a 1974 survey of sandwich graduates who had studied chemical engineering at Bradford University, which revealed that at age 27 they were earning 15 per cent more than the national norm (as assessed by a concurrent national survey sponsored by the Institute of Chemical Engineers); and, far from the early inequalities of sandwich training equalling out over the years, this percentage advantage had increased to 30 per cent at age 32. What remains unclear however, when comparing this with the Daniel and Pugh study, is whether this wage-earning superiority was due to their sandwich training, their university education or both.

A second relevant finding from this research is the discovery that the benefit of the sandwich training lies not so much in the integration of education and practical experience - which was rated low by most sandwich students - as in the sheer, first-hand exposure to the realities of industrial life during placements. This, it seems, equips the graduate with more realistic expectations concerning the types of work and peoplethey are likely to encounter at work. Third, satisfaction with the first job is about the same for sandwich and non-sandwich students whether they were trained at university or polytechnic. What this unexpected finding seems to suggest is that despite all the differences between the three sample groups in terms of their education, an overriding and unspecified factor causes them to experience a similar level of satisfaction with full-time employment. From the other evidence accrued by the study this conclusion is unconvincing. Perhaps the problem lies in the method of measurement. Daniel and Pugh tabulate ratings of various qualities sought in jobs by respondents; elsewhere they give an overall indication of job satisfaction, and also the attitudes and practices of 45 business graduate employers are recorded on a general level. But there is no attempt to correlate these separate findings and no specific details are given concerning the respective employers that graduates in the sample joined. Hence the sources of dissatisfaction for individuals cannot be explored. It may well be that sandwich and non-sandwich, university and polytechnic graduate entrants experience disenchantement at different levels and for different reasons but such nuances are hidden behind the generalised measure of satisfaction.

A further comment about this research concerns the comparison groups. The first comparison between university business graduates who are full-time, and CNAA polytechnic graduates who are exclusively sandwich trained, reveals differences which are largely explained by the educational institution rather than the merits or demerits of sandwich training. Indeed, employers in the survey openly admitted to attaching more importance in selection to general qualities like initiative and social skills, which predisposed them to prefer university job applicants. The other comparison holds institution constant and monitors the progress of CNAA business studies' students alongside those who studied CNAA economics. The latter group, it is foumd, fare less favourably in employment and this time it can be attributed, at least in part, to the superiority in employers' eyes of sandwich trained employees.

However there is one comparison not covered by this analysis, and that is how well university sandwich students cope with initial employment compared to their full-time university counterparts. What is needed, then, is a study which traces the early employment experience of contemporary cohorts of sandwich and non-sandwich university graduates.

WHY CONDUCT THIS STUDY?

The above review of graduate follow-up studies strongly suggests that the early dissatisfaction and high turnover is linked to unrealisticaly high expectations typical of graduate entrants into industrial employment. The traditional approach to assessing and explaining this supposed link between work expectations and job responses has been to take some measure of the accuracy of pre-entry expectations and investigate the impact of this variable upon job satisfaction, and ultimately, turnover. Hence, in monitoring an organization for the major symptoms of ineffective recruitment Wanous (1980) advocates collecting data concerning the expectations of outsiders to an organization, and the same individual's description of the job and company after he has commenced employment, and to relate this comparison to his reported attachment to the organisation:

> Organizations need to be able to identify those specific areas in which individuals have inflated expectations, so it is very important that expectation confirmation be measured. Just asking newcomers how satisfied or committed they are does not provide this detailed information.
> (Wanous 1980 p 46).

In terms of methodology this statement echoes the earlier conclusion of Ward and Athos (1972). They recommended that future studies of graduate recruitment, testing the discrepancy with reality hypothesis, should obtain not only the specific expectations of each entrant, but also an indication of his needs and desires as he begins work, and preferably the relative intensity of such needs. It is in response to the above suggestions of these authors that the research design adopted here was originally formulated, as explored in chapter two. However, elsewhere Wanous (1979) has admitted the shortcomings of such an approach and the need for a more integrated conceptual overview of the entire process of organizational entry, which incorporates the relevant contributions of other disciplines, including organizational and social psychology.

One such recent attempt to introduce a psychological perspective to the understanding of newcomers coping with an unfamilar work environment is that of Louis (1980). Her criticism of previous expectations literature is its implicit assumption that recruits behave in a wholly rational manner, and she calls for a more process-orientated treatment of the antecedents to recruit turnover; specifically she states:

> .....the narrow view of unmet expectationsadopted in earlier research should be broadened in future . In addition the separate effects of initial and

> disconformed expectations and overmet as well as
> undermet expectations should be assessed. Future
> research is also needed to explore the under-lying
> psychological processes by which expectations and
> surprise in general, affect individuals.
> (Louis 1980 p 246)

While these comments help to identify the refinements
required of an expectations instrument (refinements which
were subsequently incorporated in this research) they also
alert the reader to other less rational aspects of the job
entry transition. So in chapter three we ask: how do the
circumstances and social context prevailing at the time the
decision was made to join the company, together with the
outcome of that choice, affect the individual's job
attitudes? Such questions are addressed by Salancik and
Pfeffer (1978) in their social information processing
perspective. They report a number of studies which
illustrate the efficacy of their model, but they also note
that many are laboratory experiments and high on the agenda
for future research, they maintain, is the need to explore
the implications and application of the insufficient
justification research to field settings, 'since it
highlights the differences between social information
processing and needs models' (1978 p 241).

Of the field investigations that have followed, the
longitudinal study by O'Reilly and Caldwell (1981) on the
satisfaction and commitment of MBA graduate employees is one
of the most recent and relevant. They account for both
retrospective and prospective processes in their approach,
concluding that their findings are more compatible with a
theory of post-action justification, although they add:

> '... it should be noted that the findings of this
> study leave unexplained a substantial amount of
> variance, which may well be attributable to
> prospectively rational considerations' (1981 p 614).

Thus the independent and interactive impact of both sets of
factors upon the behaviours and attitudes of new employees
remains a fertile area of enquiry. The application of such a
study to the employment of graduates in the UK would in
itself be valuable, and the increasing competitiveness of the
graduatelabour market in this country brings the social
context of job choice into even sharper relief, since this
tends to enlarge the autonomy and 'strategic choice' of the
organization while diminishing the individual's perceived
freedom of choice. (Windolf 1982 p 90).

To summarise, recent available literature on graduate job entry points to a number of unresolved research issues. While it appears that graduate disenchantment can to a large extent be accredited to unrealistically high expectations prior to full-time employment, a precise method of measuring realism and relating this to a subject's job response is not yet proven. Furthermore there is increasing evidence that factors other than the content and discrepancy of work expectations influence the newcomer's assessment or 'attitude statement' concerning the job and organization. It seems that the degree to which the individual exercises autonomy in choosing his job can have a significant bearing on his future satisfaction and commitment; and while this has been tested with a sample of MBA graduates in the US, the effects of such constraints upon UK graduates has not yet been explored, nor has the investigation of expectations and job choice factors where both are independent variables yet been attempted.

NOTES

(1) However CNAA are having to accept revised proposals for three year courses. Placement of sandwich students has proved difficult, especially for overseas students.

(2) A socio-technical systems approach is one that attempts to analyse inter-dependencies between technical aspects of the work itself and the broader social milieu in which the work is done.

In an effort to assess how perceptions change during organizational entry Wanous (1976) monitored the progress of MBA students as they enrolled with three New York business schools. He did this by securing the expectations of students in the summer prior to entry, and then two descriptions of the schools they had joined, once as newcomers - one to three months after entry - second as insiders, about six months later. Although intended as a longitudinal survey only 10 per cent of all subjects had repeated measures, so the study became cross-sectional. He found that the effects of organizational entry were to bring about a lowering of original expectations for intrinsic job and organization features, such as quality of teaching, chances for personal growth and so on, but not for extrinsic factors which were more stable and identifiable, and therefore more readily anticipated.

Wanous constructed a similar study of telephone operators (Wanous 1976) over a shorter time period, spanning pre-entry to three months after entry into the employing company. He discovered, from 46 remaining operators in his sample, that once again satisfaction with job features – this time both intrinsic and extrinsic – dropped markedly over the brief employment period.   It seems conclusive, then, that this transition process does effect the perceptions of new entrants, changing naive expectations to realistic beliefs. A weakness, however, of cross-sectional studies that compare different outsider, newcomer and insider perceptions – as Wanous himself points out elsewhere (1977) – is that they cannot account for the change in the organization itself brought about by the new employee influx; this is especially true of his business school sample where there is a wholesale annual entry and exit of students, which would concomitantly change the climate and environment of the college.

2 Expectations

Prior to commencing employment new recruits have a mental picture of what the new job and company will be like. What are the effects of these expectations on their behaviour and attitudes once they have joined, and is their level of satisfaction connected to this pre-entry picture? These questions will be addressed in this chapter. To set the scene, however, it is timely to ask how it is that the expectations of company and recruit are so typically mismatched.

The views held by many graduates on various aspects of the recruitment process have already been reported (Parsons and Hutt 1981; Atton 1982; Hill 1969), and there is no doubt that unrealistic expectations can be unwittingly, or even consciously, fostered through impressions conveyed by companies' representatives and literature. Ward and Athos (1972) found a high correlation between expectations of 378 students and the job descriptions given by recruiters, which they attributed to the influence of recruiters on graduate perceptions. Posner (1981) specifically explored opinion congruence between recruiter and student perceptions, in addition to that of faculty. There was a fairly high agreement by the three parties on which job applicant characteristics were important to recruiters as generally effective in providing them with a clear understanding of the job opening and organization. The overall recruitment situation seems to be one of shared stereotypes, which in fact inhibit rather than promote realism.

To some extent, of course, unanticipated aspects of work are inevitable for the new employee entering an unfamiliar subcultural setting, and this experience of 'surprise' (Louis 1980) is probably greater for the average graduate whose education has prepared him technically, rather than emotionally and psychologically for adapting to the world of work, together with implicitly cultivating high optimism for career prospects (Schein 1964; Schein 1978).

By asking both graduates and their supervisors about 29 separate items of mutual expectations, Kotter (1973) was able to actually identify the areas of greatest mismatch. For instance, graduates were more interested in exchanging non-people related skills, such as technical knowledge and drive, for exciting, challenging and meaningful work, and development opportunities; while the organization expected to give the individual less of that which he anticipated most, and expected to receive, in addition to skills, more on such items as conformity, loyalty and so on. Kotter maintains that this divergence in expectations between existing managers and new graduates could be reconciled by explicit, frank discussion of what he calls the 'psychological contract' prior to or early in the newcomer's career; however this is hindered at the recruitment stage by the norms surrounding the interview and initial work period which define some items as not legitimate to talk about. Indeed in a 'selling' situation where both parties often quite deliberately conceal their shortcomings and emphasise their strengths, misperceptions are bound to arise (Porter, Lawler and Hackman 1975 p 134).

THE NATURE AND EFFECT OF EXPECTATIONS

In their attempts to interpret the impact of expectations researchers have adopted assorted theoretical frameworks, if any; chosen different dependent variables to correlate with levels of expectations, although most include rate of turnover; and used various intervention points in the process of organizational entry at which to collect data. This third criterion, that of chronology, provides a convenient means of ordering and assessing what might loosely be called the expectations research.

Pre-entry analysis

The one exploration of student perceptions of companies prior to employment was conducted by Ward and Athos (1972) among business school graduates from Harvard, who were either seeking a job in business or had already accepted such a job. Using a 'Common Company Description' measure, covering over 200 organizational and job features reduced to 14 factors, they were able to compare student expectations with recruiters' average descriptions of the company. When matched by companies there was a correlation between the two scores, indeed when two recruiters from the same companies were asked to describe it they did so 'in such a way that the company itself only accounted for one third of their shared descriptions. In other words, two-thirds of what they agreed on could be called a stereotype.' (p 83). This study provides fascinating data on the development of student preconceptions of work and illustrates how unrealistic expectations arise, but its value is limited because, apart from some general turnover figures which do not correlate with the measure of congruent descriptions, no post-entry data is collected in order to assess changes in attitudes over the transition period.

Further, taking the recruiter's company description as 'reality', against which to compare congruency of trainees' views does not appear to be a reliable predictor of job attitudes for two reasons. First, as Ward and Athos discovered, a large part of the recruiter's view is an unreal stereotype. Second there is no way of ensuring that any insider's (in this case the recruiter's) description is a representative reflection of organizational life. The only methodology that would circumvent this problem is to match a graduate's company perceptions, together with his work goals and needs, before entry against the reality of his own self-reported work experience some time later. Admittedly, the latter is likely to be as untypical as that of the recruiter's description, but at least the subject remains constant, and the researcher would elicit an accurate measure of discrepancy between pre- and post entry; and it is this perception after all, that will bring about feelings of dissatisfaction rather than objectively defined aspects of the organization.

Post-entry analysis

The next group of studies to be reviewed are those that question respondents at one point in time after they have joined their organization. Each study has been motivated by a desire to understand why people leave, whether they be women clerical workers (Frederico, Frederico and Lundquist 1976), military recruits (Mobley, Hand, Baker and Meglino

1979) or college graduates (Dunette, Arvey and Banas 1973; Hill 1973; Kotter 1973), and each also introduces expectations as one factor in the turnover process. The highly optimistic expectations of graduate students uncovered by Ward and Athos (1972) is a finding substantiated by the studies of graduate employees by Dunette et al (1973) and Hill (1973). Both are descriptive accounts, not based on any explicit theoretical framework, although Dunette et al did employ a modified version of Vroom's (1966) work motivation model in order to derive a motivation index for each individual, and Hill attributed his hypotheses to the research work of the Tavistock Institute of Human Relations.

Dunette et al surveyed the expectations and experiences of 1,000 graduates who either were currently employed or had been employed by Ford Motor Company (US), all with up to four years tenure. Hill's study comprised 1,600 graduates, together with 149 bosses, most of whom had been employed by Shell (UK and Netherlands) for up to ten years; 98 had left during that period, and 252 had declined an offer from Shell when graduating. Despite these differences the methodology and conclusions of the two studies are very similar. Ford 'stayers' and 'leavers' were asked to rate the importance of a number of job features, indicate their expectation of finding such features in the company, and finally to score their satisfaction with these same items, in their first and present jobs (for leavers this would have been their job with the new company). Hill utilised a similar approach with a larger number of job features (27) but failed to itemise satisfaction scores specific to Shell. In both studies a significant discrepancy emerged between what graduates had hoped for at work, and in the Ford case had definitely expected, and what they actually experienced some years later; and this gap was particularly pronounced for those who had subsequently left. The deduction made was that unmet expectations were a primary factor in voluntary turnover. Indeed Hill went on to ask 'stayer' and 'leaver' graduates to select the most important reasons why graduates leave Shell from a given list of 17; four of the five most mentioned reasons were also job features perceived as among the least congruent with expectations; the fifth reason being 'attractive outside offer'.

These two large samples of graduates provide abundant information concerning post-entry attitudes and motivation, but to then compare this data with the scores and rankings of recollected expectations prior to employment is an unsatisfactory method of assessing change. First there is the difficulty of accurately recalling perceptions of several years previously that has been mentioned above: for instance Hardin (1965) found that remembered changes in job satisfaction correlated only 0.28 with change as measured by two separatequestionnaires over a six month period. Then, as Wanous points out (1976), individuals will tend towards self-consistency in reporting pre-entry expectations when this data is solicited at the same time as evaluations of the present work situation. It is hardly surprising that those who have subsequently left the company will rate it less favourably than those who are still employees since this presumably constitutes part of their justification for seeking work elsewhere.

Other studies have also highlighted this discrepancy between expectations and work experience and then related it to turnover data collected at a different point in time. Part of the role-choice study of attrition amongst 1,500 Marine Corps recruits by Mobley et al (1979) included measures of expectancy gathered along with demographic details, immediately prior to their training. It was found that when this pre-training data was correlated with subsequent turnover 11 weeks later, those who quit (12 per cent of the total) had had lower expectations on at least two variables: expectancy of completing their enlistment and finding an acceptable civilian role, and pre-recruit training - together accounting for 10 per cent of variance in attrition. This led the authors to recommend the provision of realistic expectations prior to training in order to enhance completion rates.

Frederico et al (1976) secured the personal work details of 96 women clerical workers from a random dample of 300 who had voluntarily left one company between 1966-1974. It appeared that the less the discrepancy between initially expected salary and finally achieved salary, the less likely they would be to leave: that is, met salary expectations were significantly related to employee turnover. However the method used here for gleaning data from personnel folders is appropriate only for assessing changing expectations concerning more concrete job facets, since attitudes relating to responsibility and feelings of achievement could not be gathered easily and reliably from written records alone. And yet it is the extrinsic features of work like salary level and working conditions which are most likely to conform to original expectations anyway (Dunette et. al 1973; Wanous 1976): the areas of prior expectations most likely to change during the course of work experience are also the most elusive to measure. It must also be said that both Mobley et al (1979) and Frederico et al (1976) are measuring the maturation of expectations amongst their respondents during tenure, rather than the effect on expectations of organizational entry. The Marine Corps recruits and the female clerical workers were already insiders in their respective organizations before attitudes were tapped.

A further variation on the post-entry observation of expectations as they influence job satisfaction and turnover is provided by Kotter (1973). Rather than comparing an individual's expectations with his actual work experience, he hypothesised that the greater the match between what the individual and the company expect to give to and receive from each other, the more satisfied the new employee would be. This match derives from the concept of a psychological contract, covering a host of expectations ranging from type of technical skill required to willingness to conform to company values. The findings, based on a sample of 90 middle-managers, aged between 23 and 45 years, showed that those who had established a 'contract' that was comprised of more matches in expectations had a more satisfying and productive first year and remained longer with their company. If both parties understood their own expectations and especially if the new man discussed explicitly mutual expectations with a company employee, like his boss, there was a higher probability of a successful match.

Moreover it was found that mismatches that gave more than a person expected caused as many problems as those which yielded less. Unfortunately Kotter gives no further details of research procedure, instrument measures or analysis. The age, tenure and work experience of the sample is left vague and the impact of matched expectations on job satisfaction, productivity and turnover is outlined on a diagram but not analysed in precise terms.

Post-entry, longitudinal analysis

Finally in this section two longitudinal studies of the evolution of post-entry expectations will be reviewed. The first was a descriptive follow-up of 274 college recruits who joined American Telephone and Telegraph Company (A.T.T.) in 1956, 1957, 1959 and 1960 (Bray, Campbell and Grant 1974). This was a unique study monitoring job performance, promotions and attitudes over their first eight years with the company (107 dropped out of the sample during this time, primarily due to turnover). As with other research of college graduates (Hill 1969; Dunette, Arvey and Banas 1973; Ward and Athos 1972; O'Brien and Dowling 1978), initial expectations of work were found to be unrealistically high.

Lack of realism indicated by the correlation (0.87) between two measures: what graduates wanted in a job, and what they expected at A.T.T. The hollowness of this optimism is borne out by their attitudes towards the company which declined steadily over the seven year period for both high and low performers. What this study gains in its breadth and duration it lacks in finer detail. Forinstance, although new employees described their expectations using a 56 item 'Expectations Inventory', responses were pooled as percentages for the total group, and results for specific job facets were not reported. Also job attitudes were measured by asking respondents to think ahead to five years time with the company, rather than asking for current perceptions which would perhaps have given a more accurate picture.

Katzell (1968) used two questionnaires in her study of 1,800 nurses to identify factors in drop out during training at 43 schools of nursing. The first, measuring expectations, concerning satisfaction and stress items, were administered during their first week at school. The second, recording experience of the same items was collected eight months later, along with turnover data at one year. Low, but significant correlations were obtained between withdrawal and experienced dissatisfactions, and also between staying and confirmation of expectations. However, again, no specific results were reported on the size or direction of discrepancies between these expectations and subsequent perceptions.

In summing up the value of the above studies, it could be said that they provide an extensive but incomplete picture of the effect of expectations. It seems undeniable that initial work expectations of employees are typically inflated when compared with organizational reality, whether this 'reality' be the perceptions of recruiters (Ward and Athos 1972), the psychological contract anticipated by company managers (Kotter 1973), or the subsequent job experience of the employees themselves, measured by retest (Katzell 1968), reference to personnel data at another time (Frederico et al 1976; Mobley et al 1979) or regular monitoring (Bray et al 1974).

However, for the purposes of this research, all these studies have a common weakness: the collection of data does not take place until after entry into the organizations, even though, in some cases, this was just a few days after entry, so that what is being assessed is the effect of organizational life on the expectations of an insider. This is, naturally, a valid research objective, yielding further insights into the process and influence of socialisation; however many authors claim to be illuminating the influence of expectations on future work attitudes, and this serves to confuse rather than clarify our understanding of the antecedents to job satisfaction and turnover. Neither a dimly remembered and since distorted retrospection, nor even the evidence of newly recruited employees, constitutes a sound measure of prior expections: the first because it is too distant to be accurate, the secondbecause it will inevitably be coloured by organizational climate, even if collected on the first day with the company. The only methodology which distinguishes between the effects of prior expectations and the effects of organizational socialisation is that which solicits information from recruits before they enter the company. It is only by making this distinction that areas of incongruency can be identified and practical applications to company recruitment and induction procedures be made.

A few studies have, in fact, adopted a research design which attempts to traverse this transition, and this leads us on to the final part of our review dealing with the nature and effect of expectations.

Pre- to post-entry, longitudinal

Only two empirical longitudinal studies are known to the author where the level of expectations is measured prior to organizational entry and then correlated with post-entry variables. Schneider (1975a) hypothesised that the fit of expectations to organizational characteristics would be an important variable for predicting employee success and tenure with the company. His sample was comprised of 914 prospective insurance agents; a measure of their expectations was secured by a questionnaire sent, with the agency's formal contract, some time before they started work with the company; this tapped six broad factors of organizational climate. A measure of 'fit', or congruency, was then calculated betwen this and the climate-perceptions of agency managers, and those of old agents, constituting organizational reality. One year later performance (in terms of sales) and tenure data for the new agents was collected, but there was virtually no correlation with the pre-entry measure of expectations, except in one cluster of 'positive' type of agencies. One interesting feature of this work is the attempt to conceptualise expectations on an organizational climate level, capturing prospective employees' perceptions of the more general ethos, apart from anticipations of specific job features alone. However, Schneider speculates that it is because his Agency Climate

Questionnaire assesses general organizational characteristics rather than kinds of rewards to be obtained, which would be more directly relevant to the matching process, that no correlations emerge. There is the further possibility that, regardless of how well a person may fit a particular organisation, his probability of success may still be poor due to other, unmeasured variables. This suggests that, as noted previously, congruency between an outsider's expectations and his own subsequent work experience as an insider might be a more helpful predictor of work attitudes and performance than comparing expectations with the perceptions of existing job incumbents.

A further comment concerns the expectations reported by prospective insurance agents. Presumably most of them would have had previous work experience, most likely with other insurance agencies which would have inevitably biased their climate perceptions of the new company. Surely a more precise, less 'contaminated' way of assessing the impact of the realism of prior expectations would be to select a sample without previous work experience, or at least to account for this as a control variable? Furthermore, Schneider recommends that future research investigates the role of both expectations and preferences, since his data suggests that each may have independent effects, albeit in different situations.

In an effort to assess how perceptions change during organizational entry Wanous (1976) monitored the progress of MBA students as they enrolled with three New York business schools. He did this by securing the expectations of students in the summer prior to entry, and then two descriptions of the schools they had joined, once as newcomers (one to three months after entry) second as insiders, about six months later. Although intended as a longitudinal survey only 10 per cent of all subjects had repeated measures, so the study became cross-sectional. He found that the effects of organizational entry were to bring about a lowering of original expectations for intrinsic job and organization features, such as quality of teaching, chances for personal growth and so on, but not for extrinsic factors which were more stable and identifiable, and therefore more readily anticipated.

Wanous constructed a similar study of telephone operators (Wanous 1976) over a shorter time period, spanning pre-entry to three months after entry into the employing company. He discovered, from the 46 remaining operators in his sample, that once again satisfaction with job features, this time both intrinsic and extrinsic, dropped markedly over the brief employment period. It seems conclusive, then, that this transition process does effect the perceptions of new entrants, changing naive expectations to realistic beliefs. A weakness, however, of cross-sectional studies that compare different outsider, newcomer and insider perceptions, as Wanous himself points out elsewhere (1977), is that they cannot account for the change in the organization itself brought about by the new employee influx; this is especially true of his business school sample where there is a wholesale annual entry and exitof students, which would concomitantly change the climate and environment of the college, which in turn would influence students' perceptions. Nevertheless, the method employed in these studies, measuring pre-entry expectations and post-entry descriptions on an identical set of task-focused items, does provide a more accurate assessment of the impact of organizational entry, which can then be correlated with scores for job satisfaction.

One further longitudinal study which has partial relevance to this research area is that conducted by Ullman and Gutteridge (1974). They gathered data on the extent of job research among 251 graduating students from one university and followed up the same sample one to three years later. One of the measures of initial job search was knowledge of the company inverviewed, which is roughly equivalent to realism of expectations, and this correlated significantly with two second stage indices: subsequent satisfaction with career progress and second, tenure with initial employer. This finding lends further support to the previously reviewed evidence that pre-entry expectations are indeed a determinant of post-entry attitudes and behaviour.

Experiments

In addition to the above field studies on the nature and effects of expectations, a number of experiments have been carried out over the last 25 years, beginning with the pioneering work of Weitz (1956) with life insurance agents, which have contrasted realistic and traditional (where the information given to job candidates is often less than realistic) strategies. These have already been comprehensively reported by Wanous (1977; 1980) so some of the key findings and methods will be summarised below.

The so called 'realistic job preview' has been presented in a variety of ways: as a work sample test, as an audio visual or oral presentation, and in the form of a booklet. Some were given to prospective employees before the company offer, some after, but in all cases prior to actual entry into the organization. Of the five experiments that examined the impact of the organization's ability to recruit newcomers, all five found that presenting a realistic view of the company had no negative impact. However its effects on post-entry variables was more equivocal: six studies looked at job attitudes and of these one half found the realistic recruits more positive than the control group, but three found no difference. Twelve of the experimental studies evaluated the influence of realisticrecruitment on job turnover and nine found that, over tenure periods ranging from four weeks to one year, job survival was longer for realistic recruits; three did not reveal clear, significant differences in turnover. This could be a function of the sample type and size, as Reilly, Tenopyr and Sperling (1979) point out, suggesting\ that job previews may have more impact for more complex jobs, rather than repetitive type jobs where the amount of new information that a job preview can transmit is limited. Also, the studies successful in predicting turnover were those of a large average sample size, giving greater statistical power to detect differences in turnover. A final aspect of these experiments is that they rely on inferred measures, such as turnover, to measure changes in expectation. Reilly et al (1979) call for future research to use a more direct assessment of candidates' expectations.

Having reviewed the field studies and experimental literature on the effect of expectations on employee attitudes, it has been established that not only do new employees typically have inflated expectations concerning the job and organization they are joining, but also this lack of realism appears consistently to influence subsequent job satisfaction and voluntary turnover.

THE RELATIONSHIP OF EXPECTATIONS TO JOB SATISFACTION

Before leaving this topic, two questions need to be examined more closely. First, what psychological processes underlie this relationship: why should the level of an individual's work expectations influence his attitude towards that job? Second, what methodology suitably tests this hypothesised relationship?

Theoretical explanations

Various explanations have been put forward as to why realism tends to enhance job satisfaction and tenure. Most commonly accepted has been the 'met expectations' hypothesis (Porter and Steers 1973; Mobley, Hand, Meglino and Griffith 1979), which argues that dissatisfaction and turnover result from disconfirmed expectations, similar to a broken promise effect, as reported in work on product performance ratings (Oliver 1977). However authors, including some reviewed above, have operationalised this hypothesis in one of two ways, and although they are still treated together in some expectations studies (Dugoni and Ilgen 1981), it is less confusing to distinguish the two when examining how they have been tested.

One strand of research speaks of the unrealistic expectations of prospective and new employees as the crucial factor (Ward and Athos 1972; Bray, Campbell and Grant 1974; Wanous 1977). This argument runs as follows: pre-entry realism will lower a newcomer's initial expectations; lower expectations are more likely to be met on the job than higher, more optimistic expectations and met expectations lead to satisfaction which in turn leads to lower voluntary turnover.

Other researchers have referred to unmet expectations, emphasising the discrepancy between what entrants expected in their new job and what they actually found (Katzell 1968; Dunette, Arvey and Banas 1973; Ross and Zander 1957): in this case low satisfaction and turnover is attributed to individuals experiencing less of something desirable than was originally anticipated. Although these two theories account for most of the research in this area, other explanations have been suggested. For instance, some argue that realism has positive effects because it improves the new employee's ability to cope with the new job (Wanous 1977; Ilgen and Seely 1974). Being made aware of problems that he will encounter on the job, it is reasoned, will help prepare him for the unpleasant realities of organizational life and thus facilitate swifter, less painful adjustment. Wanous (1980) likens this to a medical vaccination, whereby a small dose of the virus is given to a patient thus enabling him to resist the disease in the future. This accords with other evidence that people are less disturbed by problems about which they have been forewarned (Finkelman and Glass 1970). Two further possible explanations, offered by Wanous (1977; 1980) relate expectations to the choice process. One is that realism concerning the various employment options facing a candidate enable him to match his needs more accurately to what the chosen company has to offer, although Schneider (1975a) found that this fit between prospective insurance agents and their new company did not relate to turnover. The other is that realism creates a perception of candidness, which helps applicants to feel less external pressure and greater autonomy in their final choice of company; this in turn presumably brings about a greater commitment once the decision is made. The last linkage in this argument is supported by applications of dissonance theory to graduate job choice (Vroom 1966; O'Reilly and Caldwell 1981).

The second question concerning the above five explanations, which are not necessarily mutually exclusive, is how can they actually be tested? What methodology is required to demonstrate the validity of one or all of these expectations hypotheses?

Increases realism

The way to test this explanation is to explore the various links within it. The first link is that realistic job previews lower expectations; this was found to be the case in five experiments that measured the impact of realistic recruitment reported by Wanous (1980). The second link is between expectations and job satisfaction. As previously discussed, very little reliable data has been collected on this: partial support is provided by Ullman and Gutteridge (1974) in their study relating realism derived from thorough job search to later job satisfaction, but in a deliberate evaluation of this relationship Dugoni and Ilgen (1981) failed to find any correlation. The final link between low job satisfaction and voluntary turnover is well established (eg. Porter and Steers 1973; Muchinsky and Tuttle 1979); and the further direct correlation between expectations and turnover is also well documented by Wanous (1977; 1980). Thus the crucial linkage of this hypothesis, the correlation between expectations and job satisfaction, is yet to be adequately demonstrated.

Reduces discrepancy

The method for testing this hypothesis has been to shift the focus from pre-entry realism to post-entry data and to point out the gap between expectations and experience on various features of the job and organization (Katzell 1968; Dunette et al 1973).

In these studies it was unmet expectations, rather than the level of initial expectations, that were associated with turnover. However, in testing this argument authors have relied upon a comparison between an individual's perception of his job and a remembered assessment of his original work expectations. A less distorted measure of matching would be between pre-entry expectations and post-entry experience on

27

the same job items. The ensuing incongruency could then be correlated with job satisfaction and turnover, providing a more accurate measurement of unmet expectations.

Improves ability to cope

Studies that measured the effect of realism, found that expectations deflated as anticipated after entry (Wanous 1980). However whether this then enables new employees to cope better than those with less realistic expectations has only been tested explicitly by Dugoni and Ilgen (1981). They did find a significant difference in the reported ability of experimental and control groups to handle difficult situations, but in the opposite direction to that predicted.

Facilitates a better choice and match

To validate this explanation, a measure needs to be taken of the job preferences or needs of all applicants, both those who accept and those who reject the company offer, in order to determine whether the match between individual needs and organizational climate is closer for the former group. If it is, then the realistic job preview can be said to positively affect job choice as a screening device. This was in fact done by Wanous (1975), and the realistic job preview was found to have no such impact. Because of the practical difficulty of collecting data from job applicants who subsequently decline jobs with the company, this hypothesis has not been pursued in this research.

Communicates honesty

Once again Dugoni and Ilgen (1981) have investigated this as a psychological explanation of job satisfaction among 119 recruits to a large retail company. Their measure simply consisted of 11 items asking respondents to what extent they felt the company was open and honest toward them. There was no significant difference between those who had received a realistic job preview and those who had not.

A QUESTION OF REALISM

From the above discussion it could be concluded that realism of expectations prior to entry does effect post-entry satisfaction and turnover, although some studies fail to find such a correlation. More questionable are the psychological reasons behind this impact, together with the methodologies used to demonstrate it.

The most promising explanation still seems to flow from the two strands of the 'met expectations' hypothesis, namely both the level of prior work expectations and subsequent disconfirmation are important elements in predicting attitudes and behaviour of new employees; it appears to the author that these two explanations are not mutually exclusive and so both will be tested in this research: by measuring pre-entry expectations and job preferences and by comparing these with post-entry perceptions of similar job and orgaizational features. The other suggested explanations that realism communicates honesty and/or enhances ability to cope and thus improves job satisfaction, though logically reasonable, have receivedsparse empirical support, and will not be tested here.

The primary way of operationalising realistic expectations in the literature has been through the use and manipulation of realistic job previews (RJPs). This, in the view of the author, has several shortcomings. The content of most RJPs have referred more to organizational expectations, that is factors common to larger aspects of the company, such as the compensation system and work procedures, than to job expectations, or those aspects specific to one job like the type of work performed, relationship with colleagues and superior and so on (Wanous 1978). It would seem important not to neglect these latter 'micro' expectations when assessing realism, since negative reaction to specific job features is likely to lead to job dissatisfaction, no matter how accurate macro climate perceptions turn out to be.

The other area of expectations that RJPs do not account for are the wider influences of the recruitment process : such things as the company's reputation and image, the quality of prior contact with the organization through its brochures, interviews and plant visits, perceptions of the company held by family and friends, and so on. All these influences would surely impinge on the reality of pre-entry expectations and yet a RJP would not necessarily incorporate or tap this broader dimension. Furthermore Louis (1980) raises doubts about appropriate subject matter for RJPs in defining what is, and what is not, realistic information and points out the inconsistencies between RJP studies : of seven studies, four were successful in showing that RJPs made significant differences to turnover, but three did not (Farr, O'Leary and Bartlett 1975; Wanous 1975; Reilly, Tenopyr and Sperling 1979). Given these uncertainties of RJP experiments, together with the field nature of the present study, which does not allow for controlled manipulation, the research design here will utilise subjects' own assessment of the job and company

they are entering as an indicator of realism: predicting
that the more accurate their pre-entry expectations are the
more likely it is that new graduates will be satisfied
employees. In addition, taking up the point voiced by
Reilly, Tenopyr and Sperling (1979), a re-measure of original
expectations will be taken after entry, rather then relying
solely on measures that indirectly assess changes in
expectations, like turnover.

However, the final and most fundamental inadequacy of the
realistic expectations hypothesis, whatever the methodology
employed to test it, concerns the psychological reasoning at
its root. The underlying premise is that a person's
disenchantment with the new job, often leading to
earlydeparture, is brought about by a failure on the part of
either the individual or the organization to anticipate the
needs and expectations of the new employee :

> 'It is assumed that newcomers are rational beings
> who enter unfamilar organizational settings with
> preformed conscious expectations about their new jobs
> and organizations, which, if met, lead to satisfaction
> and, if unmet, lead to voluntary turnover'.
> (Louis 1980 p 229).

Increasingly this assumption of volitionality in the
organization entry process has been questioned from those who
argue that future action and attitudes in the company are
likely to be shaped less by prospective expectations and more
by retrospective processes of self-justification stemming
from the original choice of job (see for instance, O'Reilly
and Caldwell 1981; Salancik 1977). This approach shifts
attention away from the content of expectations to the
circumstances surrounding, and implications following the
decision to join the organization, (O'Reilly and Caldwell
1980). The nature and impact of this job choice process as
either a confounding or complementary factor to the
rationality approach is the subject of the next chapter.

3 Organization choice

So far, in the analysis of literature which examines the antecedents to early turnover amongst graduate recruits, we have concentrated on the content and level of expectations as a factor influencing job satisfaction and tenure. The findings gathered from a wide range of descriptive, correlation and experimental studies, seem to support this hypothesis; however the evidence is neither overwhelming nor unanimous, which suggests other variables may be at play in this relationship between events and behaviour prior to job entry and those following. Furthermore, accepting that there is a correlation stemming from met expectations, there still remains the question of why this effects subsequent attitudes in the manner reported.

Part of the problem may well lie in the narrowness of this approach. To focus entirely on an individual's expectations and perception of the job reflects a psychological orientation which seeks to explain behaviour in terms of the internal dynamics of the motivation process alone. This single effect view is valid as far as it goes, but neglects the attenuations of more complex social and psychological influences: for instance, the realities of past socialisation and present circumstances leading up to job selection, and the effects of the organisational choice itself on motivation.

Secondly, as previously mentioned, the approach lacks breadth in its dependence on a model of rational decision-making, failing to account of the self-justifying behaviour which could well attend such an important choice and transition process.

A helpful way to explore the potential impact of these two related dimensions is to review the literature pertaining to organizational choice. First by taking a prospective focus and looking at the kinds of constraints and influences which help to shape expectations and precipitate choice. Second, by taking a retrospective focus and reporting on research which illuminates post choice behaviour.

PROSPECTIVE FOCUS

When coming to the literature which assesses the impact of organizational choice factors on the entry of individuals into full-time employment, there is something of a dilemma. On the one hand much has been written in the fields of vocational psychology and sociology about the process of occupational choice, but with little explicit reference to actual choice of organization. On the other hand, researchers who have examined organizational choice have concentrated almost entirely on the psychological level of how individuals choose between job options. For instance, Wanous (1977) prefaces his comprehensive review of organizational entry research by distinguishing between occupational and organizational entry: he describes the latter as an event, rather than a process, and hence concludes that 'non-psychological theories of occupational entry (economic, sociological, cultural...) are not as relevant for organizational entry' (1977 p.602). Such a distinction seems unnecessarily artificial. Yes, ultimately organizational choice is a once-in-time choice, but to treat it as an isolated decision-making event ignores the broader social context of this transition, and thus possibly overlooks the influence of important variables. Therefore, both approaches, one emphasising the psychology of decision-making, the other considering the external, social-structural aspects of occupational and organizational choice will be reviewed selectively below.

A psychological perspective of occupational choice.

If one accepts Crites' (1969) approach to vocational choice whereby from childhood, through to adulthood many choices are made, gradually eliminating the range of possible careers until an ultimate first job is decided upon, then organizational choice and entry cannot be divorced from the overall context of occupational entry. Nevertheless, comparatively few studies have focused specifically on organizational preference and choice.

The preoccupation of psychologists in this field has been with the decision-making process of individuals as they weigh up career and work preferences against available job offers. The theoretical frameworks for these studies differ but consistently the three themes of perceptions (why jobs become attractive), values (what work goals are important to the job-seeker) and opportunities (which job openings are actually feasible) emerge as the important variables.

For instance Ginzberg et al (1951), on the basis of a research project conducted amongst US high school and college students, adopt a developmental approach to occupational choice : they interpret attitudes and behaviour in terms of the maturation of an individual's innate capacities. This culminates in a stage of realistic choice when the individual attempts to effectively link up the constraints of the adult work-world with personal interests and values. This model has been criticised for failing to account for the influence of personality factors on career perceptions and choice (White 1968), for its narrow sample (Roberts 1968) and for attempting to be all-inclusive (Kuvlesky and Bealer 1966), but it nevertheless provides a helpful framework within which information about various aspects of the entry process can be coordinated (Timperley 1974).

Super (1953) builds upon this developmental approach in his theory of the role of personality in the vocational choice process. He maintains that people attempt to implement their own self-concept when choosing careers and jobs; in other words, they are attracted to those organizational roles most congruent with the image they have of themselves. Tom (1971), in his study of college students, found some support for this theory when extended to organizational choice. The similarity between profiles for self-description and the description for most preferred organizations was significantly greater than the similarity between the profiles for self-description and descriptions of least preferred companies. However, this study measured attractiveness and preference in what is essentially a hypothetical situation, since no data was collected on the congruency of actual choice and self-description profiles, or the effect of congruency on subsequent attitudes once in the organization. Hayes (1973) also utilised Super's self-concept theory in analysing UK apprentices' work perceptions; this time post-entry data was reported. On the basis of his findings he doubted whether occupational self-concept had in fact crystallised at the time of work entry: 'occupational choice and work experience could...be viewed as important contributors to the development of an occupational self-concept, rather than outcomes' (1973 p.40). This, incidentally reinforces this author's earlier assertion that extent of work experience may be a crucial variable in determining expectations and hence post-entry attitudes and behaviour. So, although questions remain about the direction and timing of the relationship between self-concept and job preference/choice, the work of Super has served to highlight the compromise between interests, values and abilities of individuals with the limitations of the real life occupational world.

These features of occupational entry have also been conceptualised by Blau, Gustad, Jenson, Parnes and Wilcox (1956). They integrate the disciplines of economics and sociology to construct a framework of occupational choice and entry which stresses the complementary processes of choice both by individual and employer, which will usually involve compromise between preference and expectations for both parties. Again, apparent in this model is the developmental nature of occupational choice - which encompasses a wide range of factors. A further refinement is made by Kuvlesky and Bealer (1966), who point out the need to distinguish conceptually aspirations from expectations, because 'the object with an expectation is an anticipated occurrence, and the individual's orientation towards their expected state may be favourable or unfavourable' (1966 p.273). For instance, a person may have an occupational aspiration to be a doctor, but knowing his parents cannot afford the expense of extended education required to meet this goal, his occupational expectations may be to become a salesman. Thus, they conceive an individual as assessing the limited factors of both the external environment and his own abilities, capacities and values as he approaches choice of occupation.

Finally, Vroom (1964), although a motivational theorist and thus concerned primarily with the internal dynamics of the decision-making process, also acknowledges the constraining features of the occupational world in his model: he views occupational choice as a function not only of valence, but also of realistic expectancy that such a work role can be attained.

A psychological perspective of organizational choice

The above studies are representative of research into the choice of occupation. The 15 or so studies which have taken organizational choice as their focus, reviewed by Wanous (1977; 1980), also isolate perceptions, values and opportunities as the salient features to an individual as he chooses a job. This is probably because the most prevalent theory in this research is expectancy theory (Vroom 1964), which maintains that the attractiveness of an organization is determined by multiplying perceived company characteristics by the desirability (valence) of those characteristics, and secondly that the degree of effort directed towards joining a chosen company is a function of the organization's attractiveness and the individual's expectation that such an effort will be rewarded by the company. In summarising the accumulated evidence for these propositions Wanous (1980) found reasonable support for expectancy theory, especially in it's ability to predict that the final choice of organization would be the one highest in 'attractiveness' from those offering a place.

However, the author's interest in this theory of organizational choice is less in what it describes and predicts, and more in what it omits to say about choice behaviour. For instance, much emphasis is put on the fact that an individual evaluates various characteristics of an organization, but we are not told why he comes to value some work features above others; further, final choice is described as a 'pay-off' between attractiveness on the one hand, and probability of achieving work goals, on the other: what such a formulation alludes to - but does not amplify - is the influence of external constraints on the final decision, such as the competition of the labour market. In fact, Herriot and Ecob (1979), in a study which attempts to answer earlier objections to decision theory, were able to explore the above two points. They investigated the intentions of 117 electrical and mechanical engineering students to undertake certain types of work in industry. Decision theory was effective in predicting occupational choice, but this success was enhanced when two additional mediating variables were included. The first was a measure of perceived social pressure, which constituted the degree to which the opinions of significant others were taken into account and the motivation to comply with these evaluations. For example, there was general perceived disapproval of jobs in sales, the armed services, nationalised industry and production, whereas design and R & D work had higher 'subjective norms' ratings. The second element which improved predictions was a variable representing the subject's estimate of how likely he was to obtain work of a particular type if he wanted it: this measure was taken to reflect both the individual's assessment of the job market and his estimate of his own capabilities. A second, similar study of final year engineering students, this time longitudinal, comprising seven questionnaires over a 14 week job-hunting period, yielded further supportive evidence for the inclusion of these two variables (Herriot, Ecob and Hutchison 1980).

Thus, in summarising the psychological approach to both occupational and organizational choice reviewed above, an expected emphasis is found on the individual, his personality, his values and his preferences. But also apparent is an often tacit recognition that external realities impinge upon choice, that expectations temper preference. Two such external constraints are noteworthy in that they have been singled out empirically as being influential in job choice (Herriot and Ecob 1979; Herriot et al 1980) : namely, the potential pressure of significant others' opinions and the realistic job opportunities presented by the labour market. The fact that these studies were analysing the behaviour and attitudes of final year students at a UK university, make the findings all the more pertinent to this research.

A sociological perspective of occupational choice.

At this point, it is worth looking at the sociological perspective of occupational choice to examine how the variables it deals with amplify and complement the above psychological formation of career decisons.

The work of Keil, Riddell and Green (1966) is of particular interest since, although they were observing 16 year old school leavers rather than graduates, their central concern was the adjustment or 'fit' between individuals and their new jobs, expressed in terms of satisfaction, new attitudes and expectations, and possible job change. They saw three groups of factors contributing to the development of work attitudes: first the socialisation of the young person to the world of work by his family, neighbourhood, school and peers (or what we might summarise as formal and informal social structures); second, previous work experience; third, the wider social influences such as media and personal religious and political affiliation. This is a useful classification, so examples of research in each of these areas will be reviewed below to assess potential impact on organizational choice.

Formal and informal structures

Roberts (1968) stresses the impact of social structures on occupational choice, focusing especially on the role of education in regulating entry to the first job. In a random survey of 196 young men in the Greater London area aged between 14-23 years, he sets out to test various hypotheses derived from the developmental theories of Ginzberg and Super. Failing to find support for these hypotheses he proposes an 'opportunity - structure' model pertaining to the British school leaver situation. Job entry, he maintains, relates strongly to administrative proximity, because academic achievements are among the main criteria used in job selection by employers, and also social proximity, because recruitment often takes place via informal channels of parents and kin:

> 'The momentum and direction of school-leavers' careers are derived from the way in which job opportunities become cumulatively structured and young people are placed in varying degrees of social proximity with different ease of access to different types of employment' (1968 p.179).

In other words, although individuals may perceive themselves to have free occupational choice, they are in fact very much restricted to a narrow range of job opportunities. This is reminiscent of Vroom (1964), who saw occupational attainment as the result of two sets of choices: a choice made by the individual, and the choice made by social institutions, implying that people are not only selecting occupations but are selected for occupations.

Although Roberts' study concerned the occupational choice of school leavers, many with limited scholastic qualifications, his emphasis on labour market opportunities has much relevance to research on the organizational choice of graduates, especially as the job openings for UK graduates in many employment sectors have become far more competitive since the peak intake year of 1978 (Parsons and Hutt 1981).

The influence of family and social class on occupational preference and choice has received much attention by sociologists, since the socio-economic position of the family, particularly the father, is seen to be a primary socialising factor (Rosenberg 1957; Kelsall, Poole and Kuhn 1970; 1972). Schools and colleges also play a vital part in the transmission of occupational values and attitudes: Kelsall et al conclude from their large postgraduate sample that family background, school and university complement each other as forces of social class, channelling those from a more privileged background into professional and managerial careers. This view is substantiated by those who have analysed the education and social origins of elites in UK society (Stanworth and Giddens 1974; Wakeford 1974); and in writing about non-advanced further education, Gleeson (1980) argues that the form, more than the content, of college training actively reinforces, rather than passively reflects, social differentiation between craft and technical apprentices.

A further factor influencing career choice is peer groups, both within and without the educational institution: the culture and work attitudes of such groups provide a source of reference, often an alternative to that of family and school, for individuals throughout their careers (Timperley 1974). Finally, the information and advice provided by the various agencies of careers guidance represent a formal channel, the influence of which should not be ignored, despite the fact that such agencies have often been criticised for their ineffectiveness in integrating employee potential with the demands of industry (Rogers and Williams 1970; Snow 1973; Pearce and Jackson 1976).

An individual's home and educational background will have a considerable influence, then, in the shaping of vocational choice, and such sociological variables will be embraced by this research; but in analysing the actual choice of organization, certain features rise to special prominence – notably, the opinions and influence of others to whom the individual refers his judgements. In most cases this would be his family and peer group friends (Sofer 1970). Indeed 68 per cent of university students profess to find friends and relatives as helpful when choosing between organizations (Williamson 1981).

The influence of work experience

Most studies in this field – as reviewed above – look at the development of occupational values and how these influence job selection, satisfaction and job change, with the underlying assumption that occupational values are formed relatively early in life and persist, largely unaltered, throughout the work history. However, a few researchers have turned this around and hypothesised that work experience itself may bring about a shift in these values, and hence a corresponding effect on future occupational choice, career development and subjective responses to work.

For instance Mortimer and Lorence (1979) carried out a ten year longitudinal study of 512 male graduates from Michigan University, focusing on the processes of occupational selection and socialisation. Using Rosenberg's (1957) three-fold values dimensions, they demonstrated that experiencing work autonomy had a significant impact on intrinsic reward values, such as 'opportunities to exercise my abilities and skills' and people-oriented values, such as 'the chance to work with people rather than things'. Also, income, a prominent extrinsic reward and indicator of occupational success, was found to enhance extrinsic values, such as 'opportunities for advancement'.

In another longitudinal survey, this time looking at 68 craft apprentices selected by the Yorkshire Electricity Board, Hayes (1973) found that over a period of 20 months the relative importance of so-called 'psycho-social' aspects of work, which included such aspects as the social work situation, company image, and life-style implications, increased considerably after a period of work experience. Further, the importance of these psycho-social aspects of the job had been definitely under estimated prior to the commencement of employment; Hayes attributes this to the tendency of careers officers to emphasise the economic and extrinsic features of work, as against the less easily identifiable intrinsic ones.

Concurring evidence comes from a further, longitudinal study of school-leavers, students, young workers and intelligensia in yet a third national setting, Estonia: Titma (1979) concludes that:

> 'Acquiring familiarity with work in the practical process of production is a most important factor in shaping orientation towards work and that in the case of young professionals the formation of this orientation is delayed during the period of studies and takes the final form only later when young people actually begin to work.' (1979 p.358)

These studies add empirical weight to the observations of Slocum (1967) made sometime ago that there is no substitute for actual work experience to provide an adolescent with an opportunity for testing his aptitudes and interests against the requirements of occupational roles.

Thus, along with the 'occupational selection hypothesis', that persons choose their work on the basis of already formed psychological characteristics, there does seem to be a case for adding that subsequent work experience can, in turn, mould aspects of personality - affecting job attitudes, behaviour and future job choice. Although the above research refers to the effects of joining full-time employment for the first time, nevertheless we would expect to find those graduates entering the job market with substantial prior work experience, to be influenced, both in the choosing of and the subsequent attachment to the chosen organization, by a more mature work orientation and a greater appreciation of otherwise overlooked psycho-social aspects of work.

Wider social influences

The third factor influencing work choice and attitudes that Keil et al (1966) mention is that of wider social influences. Once again, much research has been carried out assessing the impact of socio-economic, political and religious values on occupational choice, but little attention has been given to the effect of these variables on choice of organization despite the fact that traditional decision theory incorporates, at least by implication, the concept of individual values, or valence (eg. Vroom 1964; Vroom 1966; Vroom and Deci 1971).

In an analysis of various social and economic variables among four socio-religious groups in Detroit, Lenski (1960) demonstrated that membership of such groups had as great an influence on economic behaviour as social class: for instance white Protestants and Jews had a significantly stronger identification with the individualistic, competitive patterns of thought and action associated with the protestant ethic and its secular counterpart, the spirit of capitalism, than Catholics and negro Protestants. Greeley (1968) sought to apply this conclusion to the occupational choice of a sample of graduates whose 'original religion' was cited as either Catholic or Protestant. His hypotheses that Catholics would be less inclined to go to college and less likely to pursue an academic career in the physical sciences were not substantiated. Greeley suggested that this was due to the different ethnic characteristics between the largely Polish sample in Detroit, studied by Lenski, and his own national survey of students. There remain obvious difficulties in measuring religion as a variable: defining individuals as Protestants or Catholics may be little more than nominal labels, reflecting nothing about personal religious convictions. Lenski adopted more sophisticated criteria than official denomination alone : he ascertained detailed information about group membership, doctrinal orthodoxy and personal devotionalism and thus derived a more meaningful understanding of religious values which proved to have predictive strength.

There are similar problems in measuring political orientations, but McFalls and Gallagher (1979) attempted to relate political values to the occupational preference of 200 students and found a remarkably high differentiation between conservatives, moderates, liberals and radicals. This study, however, has several weaknesses : it is very unlikely that respondents would indicate occupational values inconsistent with their previously expressed political orientation; second, the interviews only revealed data on occupational preference and there is no record of their actual choice, which would be a more reliable and substantial variable to compare with values; third, as the authors admit, there was no control for personality attributes.

Between 1950-2 Rosenberg (1957) analysed the occupational choices and values of three separate samples of college graduates, and this work remains a classic in its field. He distinguished three basic sets of occupational values : self-expression values, people-oriented values and extrinsic reward values and then went on to demonstrate that those choosing certain occupations tended to manifest similar values. For instance, those choosing careers in social work and teaching typically rated working with people rather than things, or having opportunities to help others, as very important; to those choosing careers in engineering and science, however, these values were less important. On the other hand business careers and law were disproportionately likely to be high on extrinsic reward orientation. Further studies of students in the US and UK have revealed comparable results (Davis 1965; Mansfield and Davies 1971), though it is not clear whether values determine career choice or career choice influences values. Underhill (1966) set out to answer this question in a 10 year longitudinal study of graduates and found that it depended on the type of career being considered: for humanities and education and law, values appear stronger in influence, while for medicine, engineering and business the career choice predominates. He tied this finding in with a previous one of Rosenberg's (1957) that an individual who has invested a lot of time in preparing for a career, typical of medicine and engineering, is more motivated to bring his values into line with his career direction, because to change would be too costly. This reasoning, if valid, has significant implications for the sandwich course students in the present research, since most would have made a relatively greater undergraduate investment in certain careers than their full-time student contemporaries.

So, in summary, the research has shown fairly conclusively that an individual's personal values, whether they be expressed in social, religious, political and/or occupational form, do have an influence on choice of occupation. The strength and direction of this influence seems to vary, but in considering organizational choice it is obviously necessary to account for such values, if only as a moderating variable.

This review has also revealed that the experience of work itself exerts a powerful influence in the shaping of these values, and particularly noteworthy is the differential stability of occupational values over time for those with, and those without substantial work experience : the implications for the sample in this research, comprised of sandwich and non-sandwich graduates, is clear.

In reviewing the literature on occupational and organizational choice from both psychological and sociological perspectives, a whole range of variables have been considered ranging from individual personality factors, to organizational attractiveness and the influence of schooling and personal values. It has been shown that most of these factors have some relevance to the present study, if only in providing the framework within which specific jobs are ultimately chosen. However, a few have consistently emerged with special salience to a study of organizational choice : namely, the perceived competitiveness of the labour market, the opinions of significant others and the extent of previous work experience. Other factors are perhaps more influential in the earlier stages of occupational choice, but at the time of deciding upon a job these three appear to have crucial importance as constraining variables. Interestingly, two of these variables are among those singled out by researchers who have analysed the job choice and entry process from a retrospective focus. These studies will be examined next.

RETROSPECTIVE FOCUS

In this chapter we have been reviewing research which analyses the way people choose occupations and organizations, in order to establish which pre-entry factors are important in determining graduates' subsequent satisfaction with, and commitment to, the companies they join.

The common premise underlying all the literature so far, both psychological and sociological, together with the expectations research considered in chapter two, is that of prospective rationality. This argument assumes that behaviour flows from prior attitudes : in other words, an individual's attitude in the form of his work goals, personal values and prior expectations about the job are matched against the opportunities and requirements of the prospective employer - the closeness of this match determines his behaviour in terms of job satisfaction and desire to. stay or leave. The approach is prospective, because it relies on present attitude data to predict future behaviour; and it is rational in that it assumes the individual will make a reasonable choice based on the information available to him at the time of decision. (It is acknowledged that this will often be less than complete, but the important fact is that the individual believes he has a full grasp of the situation and thus perceives himself to be making a rational choice) (1).

Another way of interpreting this choice process and its consequences for new employees is to explain it in terms of retrospective justification, whereby an individual makes a job choice and this behaviour itself serves to constrain future actions and attitudes in, and toward, the company. This reasoning stems from several interlocking psychological theories and perspectives. In the following sections the pertinent aspects of these will be reviewed to see how they elucidate understanding of organizational choice.

Cognitive dissonance

Festinger (1957) asserts that cognitive dissonance is created when an individual chooses one alternative when faced with two or more equally attractive choices. This dissonance is aroused by the awareness of relatively unattractive properties in the chosen alternative, and relative attractive features in those not chosen.

The individual will seek to reduce his resultant post decision discomfort by perceptually distorting the relative attractiveness of the two or more alternatives, such that the chosen alternative is seen favourably and the rejected alternative(s) is seen unfavourably. In short, the individual persuades himself that he made the right decision after all, and brings his thinking into line with this previous action.

These theoretical predictions are supported by the results of laboratory experiments (Brehm 1956; Brehm and Cohen 1959; Brock 1963) and also in field studies relating to the organizational choice of graduates (Vroom 1966; Vroom and Deci 1971). In 1964 and again in 1965, Vroom collected data from 49 business management graduates immediately prior to their final job choice, and again four weeks later after they had decided on the organization they were going to work for. The results showed that students restructured the alternatives in a direction consistent with the choice they had made, such that they perceived the chosen company as more attractive and more instrumental to goal attainment after choice than beforehand; and the reverse was true of the rejected alternatives.

A follow-up study of the same students one year later and

again three and one half years later by Vroom and Deci (1971), revealed that these changed orientations towards chosen and non-chosen alternatives were no longer in evidence after implementation of choice : attractiveness for the chosen organization decreased markedly during the first year and remained low; this did not indicate regret with the earlier choice because the previously rejected alternative was described three and one half years later in even less favourable terms. Lawler, Kuleck, Rhode and Sorenson (1975) also found evidence for post choice dissonance immediately after the job choice decision, followed by a similar, general decline in perceived attractiveness for all companies one year later, in their study of 431 accounting graduates.

The significance of this dissonance effect for research dealing with organizational choice is thus apparent. The existence of other, viable job offers at the time of choosing an employer may well lead to reinforcement of positive attitudes towards the chosen job. Further, it can be said that dissonance is only likely to mediate between decisions and attitudes where the individual perceives his decision to be a free one; where a choice is influenced by external variables, possibly parental coercion or the purely instrumental motive of a high salary, it would no longer be necessary for the individual to make any cognitive re-appraisals because there is no dissonance : the reasons for choosing the job are manifest and he can divert 'blame' from himself to these external factors if the decision brings negative consequences. It might then be assumed, that having made an autonomous choice, free from external pressures, a graduate would be automatically satisfied and committed to stay with the company. However, as the follow-up studies have demonstrated (Vroom and Deci 1971; Lawler et. al 1975) disillusionment ensues, for chosen and non-chosen jobs alike; these studies do not disclose the degree of autonomy surrounding individuals' choices, but what becomes clear is that for dissonance to be aroused and for the consequent positive attitudes to be sustained toward the chosen alternative, a person must be committed to his choice. This is a particularly important facet of the job choice process to draw attention to, because some students regard their first job as a stepping stone to another future job, in which case the binding effect of the original decision would be diminished. Commitment, and its implications, is interwoven with dissonance theory but nevertheless it remains conceptually different, thus it will be dealt with separately below.

Commitment

The conception of organizational commitment most frequently encountered involves some form of psychological bond between people and organization. For instance, Buchanan (1974), in his review of this research, draws together three elements of commitment : identification with the goals and values of the company, involvement in a work role, and a sense of loyalty to the organization. Other authors include additional aspects, such as willingness to exert high levels of effort (Porter, Steers, Mowday and Boulian 1974), and not being prepared to leave the organization for increments in pay, status or professional freedom (Hrebiniak and Alutto 1972). What typifies this research is its focus on attitudinal commitment, whereby the goals of both organization and individual become increasingly congruent (Hall, Schneider and Nygren 1970). It thus reflects the prospective rationality approach which we have already discussed.

Another approach to the concept of commitment focuses on what Mowday, Steers and Porter (1979) call 'commitment related behaviours', and reflects the retrospective emphasis. Kiesler and Sakamura (1966; Kiesler 1971) were among the first to articulate a theoretical model for the role of commitment in attitude change. Their seminal definition of commitment as 'the pledging or binding of the individual to behavioural acts' (1966 p.349) effectively reverses the prospective view of organizational choice.

Two assumptions underpin this prediction : the first is that individuals attempt to resolve inconsistencies between the behaviour they perform and the attitudes they hold. Obviously, this borrows from dissonance theory (Festinger 1957). Second, the effect of commitment is to make an act or behaviour less changeable, so that people tend to continue acting in ways consistent with the implications of their past behaviours. To these, Salancik (1977) adds the third assumption that these implications of past behaviour are not given, but are invested into a situation by the individual's own beliefs or by the beliefs and expectations of others. This is integral to the social information processing approach which basically posits that work needs and attitudes are the outcome of the social context of work and the presence and consequences from previous actions rather than inherent properties of the individual as assumed by need theorists. (This approach will be discussed further below).

Kieslier and Sakamura (1966) go on to describe the circumstances under which behaviours would be more binding :

the degree of commitment would depend, they maintain, on the number of acts performed by the individual, the importance of those acts for him, the explicitness and irrevocability of the act(s) and the perceived freedom of choosing to perform the act(s). In testing one derivation of this model they found that the less pressure exerted on subjects to perform an act consistent with their beliefs, the greater the resistance to subsequent counter communications. Illustrating a further aspect, Gerard (1968), in his theory of cognitive consistency, reports on an experiment in which it was found that subjects who truly committed themselves irrevocably by giving up the unchosen alternative, showed more evidence of dissonance than subjects who simply announced a preference but who, in practical terms, did not give up the alternative.

The value of this commitment model is that it enhances prediction of organizational commitment, as against prospective models (Buchanan 1974; Mowday, Steers and Porter 1979) which are only useful after the event to classify persons as committed or not, without necessarily explaining how that commitment was created. Certainly the emphases on the need to appear consistent, the effects of external constraints, and the importance of perceived autonomy of choice are all strikingly relevant to the graduate's choice of, and transition into, full-time employment. For instance, from Kiesler's model it could be predicted that an individual choosing a company free from external pressure is likely to resist future counter-communication, perhaps in the form of colleagues' negative comments about the new workplace, and rather than doubt the wisdom of his original decision, he will retrospectively justify it and be more committed to his course of action. Thus, unlike the met-expectations hypotheses and prospective rationality approaches, this reasoning can run counter to intuition.

Insufficient justification

A further aspect deriving from the theories of dissonance and commitment which deserves special mention is the body of research which analyses the effects of insufficient justification; the argument being that when faced with inadequate reasons, in the form of extrinsic rewards, for performing a task (or in our case, joining an organization), an individual will tend to develop attitudes that rationalise their behaviour - particularly if their past choice or action is difficult to undo or reverse.

Pfeffer and Lawler (1980) elaborate this paradigm, breaking it down into two parts which are applicable to organizational

choice. First, when a job is chosen for intrinsic, as opposed
to extrinsic, reasons it is likely to result in positive
attitudes towards work. Second, once committed to an
organization an individual will be more satisfied and
committed when the extrinsic rewards or salience of them is
low. Thus the first part highlights the circumstances
surrounding the original job choice, and the second explores
the influence of post-choice factors, but both have
significant implications for the work attitudes of graduate
entrants. Research supporting these two facets of the choice
process will be evaluated below.

Intrinsic and Extrinsic Motivation

Experiments dealing with intrinsic and extrinsic motivation
show that when a decision to pursue a course of action is
freely chosen, this results in more positive attitudes and
greater persistence. Whereas the intervention of external
constraints on choice and extrinsic rewards for performance
has the opposite effect. For instance, Folger, Rosenfeld and
Hayes (1978) examined the effect of pay and choice on
productivity and intrinsic motivation, in an experiment with
50 students; they found that when subjects felt freedom of
choice to accept or reject compensation for a task, more
favourable attitudes towards the task ensured, than for those
who felt constrained to do the task. In an experiment with
pre-school children, Lepper and Greene (1975) gave the
subjects the opportunity to play with highly attractive toys
if they engaged in an activity. It was discovered that those
who had taken part in the activity expecting the extrinsic
reward showed less subsequent interest in the activity than
those who did not anticipate a reward.

The external constraint does not necessarily consist of a
reward however. In choosing to participate in a task,
individuals are likely to have positive attitudes towards it
however unpleasant the outcome, providing the original
decision was volitional rather than coerced. For instance,
Comer and Laird (1975) found students prepared to follow
through with their 'free choice' to participate in an
experiment - and comment favourably upon the task - despite
the fact that it entailed consciously eating a dead worm!
Mynatt and Sherman (1975) compared the reaction of individuals
and groups participating in acts which transpired to have
negative consequences. Individuals, whose choice was self-
determined lowered their cognitive conflict by misperceiving
the aversiveness of the outcome; whereas the group decision-
makers were able to diffuse and deny responsibility for the
outcome. If these findings can be applied to the real life

situation of graduate job choice, then the amount of autonomy exercised in that choice and the degree of influence from family and friends is going to be an important determinant of future company commitment.

A possible limitation of these, and other similar studies reviewed elsewhere (O'Reilly and Caldwell 1981) is that they are based almost exclusively on experiments with student or child samples. Pfeffer and Lawler (1980) acknowledge that student groups are likely to be naive and easily manipulated and that typically laboratory findings have shortlived effects. Nevertheless recent field studies testing the impact of the insufficient justification paradigm on behavioural commitment have largely substantiated these experimental findings.

O'Reilly and Caldwell (1980) surveyed 108 MBA graduates immediately after accepting jobs, and again six months afterwards with a view to discovering how decision factors affected subsequent job satisfaction and commitment to the companies they joined. Choice predicated on intrinsic job features of the future employer and made free from external pressures (such as family or financial considerations) was associated with greater satisfaction and commitment. However, contrary to prediction, students motivated by the extrinsic features of salary and location also expressed more positive attitudes subsequently than those not excited about these aspects of the job. Results published later (O'Reilly and Caldwell 1981) showed that job decisions perceived as less revocable were also associated with positive sentiments about the job, a finding which the authors attributed to post-choice justification. The second thread of the insufficient justification paradigm that Pfeffer and Lawler (1980) explore, concerns its interaction with commitment.

Commitment and Insufficient Justification

A field experiment, which illustrates well the interaction of these two effects, is that by Staw (1974) of Reserve Officers' Training Corps (ROTC) cadets. He found that when the threat of draft was removed those cadets not bound by a committing contract dropped out of the ROTC. However, those who were already obligated to the training programme actually rationalised their commitment and stayed with the organization: the absence of sufficient extrinsic reasons for the past decision and behaviours (joining and training with the ROTC) impelled them not only to remain but also to develop favourable attitudes towards the programme. Thus the crucial element differentiating the leavers from the stayers was prior commitment.

Closely allied to this is another facet of job choice which relates commitment to work attitudes : that of alternative job opportunities. How an individual responds to the existence of other job options is a complex issue. March and Simon (1958) and Price (1977) typify the conventional view and argue that the greater the number of alternatives available and perceived, the greater is the likelihood of voluntary termination to take up a more attractive job. However the dissonance literature reviewed above would predict the opposite : that the more choice an individual exercises in a decision, to join a company, or stay with it, the more committed he will be to that course of action, because the rejection of suitable alternatives itself constitutes an act of choice which requires self-justification (Pfeffer and Lawler 1980). However, although freedom of choice is seen as an important contribution to commitment, and therefore to the development of favourable work attitudes, another potent factor inducing commitment is that the act/decision be irrevocable (Kiesler and Sakamura 1966; Staw 1974; Salancik 1977). Thus, an individual may make a job choice from several alternatives which would suggest subsequent commitment to the decision, but paradoxically the continued existence of those same alternatives make the decision to remain with the current organization revocable - so confounding the previous favourable attitudes created by free choice.

This shows the importance of distinguishing between the presence of job alternatives at the time of organizational choice, and the salience of such alternatives after employment has begun. The impact of the latter was assessed by Pfeffer and Lawler (1980) in their analysis of a survey of university and college faculty in the US and by O'Reilly and Caldwell (1981) in their longitudinal study of MBA students. In both cases the evidence indicated that where individuals possessed insufficient extrinsic justification for their original job choice decision (perhaps because they accepted an offer at lower than average salary) the prospect of another job lowered their satisfaction and commitment to their present employer. The authors maintain that this is because receiving inquiries about other jobs suddenly causes the initial choice to be seen as reversible and the salary difference more salient: this, in turn, negatively affects attitudes toward the present company. To ascertain the availability of job alternatives both studies questioned whether job offers or serious inquiries had been received in the previous two years (Pfeffer and Lawler 1980), or since starting work (O'Reilly and Caldwell 1981). But, constructing the measure in this way ignores the suitability

of such offers and enquiries : they could have been quite
inappropriate and thus unrealistic as alternatives, so to
derive an index of revocability from this question appears
tenuous. Second, since these alternatives had previously been
rejected they do not necessarily reflect perception of
existing alternatives. Along with these methodological
comments there is a cultural consideration which renders this
aspect of these studies less relevant. Given the present
situation of the UK graduate labour market, a decision by a
student to choose a company is likely to be less revocable for
two reasons : first, the rejected alternative job offers are
unlikely to remain as viable options should he subsequently
wish to change jobs six months or one year later since
graduate supply presently exceeds demands in all but a few
sectors; second, it is unlikely that other than exceptional
graduates will actually receive job offers or inquiries
initiated by other companies, it is usually for the graduate
himself to pursue the possibility of such moves. These
factors change the nature of the 'availability of
alternatives' measure since its place in the O'Reilly et
al/Pfeffer et al research design is precisely that such offers
come unexpectedly from external sources to increase saliency
of insufficient justification which would otherwise have been
overlooked.

In summary, an individual choosing a job from several viable
alternatives has a greater perception of volitionality and
will hence be more satisfied and committed because according
to the commitment model (Kiesler and Sakamura 1966; Salancik
1977), volition enhances commitment and the insufficient
justification paradigm (Pfeffer and Lawler 1980) predicts that
such a choice which lacks sufficient extrinsic justification
also serves to increase future commitment and satisfaction.
In contrast, an employee once established in a company and
then made aware of alternative jobs will become less satisfied
and committed, since this represents revocability which has
been shown to limit behavioural commitment (Pfeffer and Lawler
1980; O'Reilly and Caldwell 1981). For the reasons outlined
above, this research project set as it is in the UK graduate
context, will be more concerned with the affects of pre-entry
circumstances surrounding organizational choice.

Social information processing approach

The value of this approach posited by Salancik and Pfeffer
(1978), and akin to the social action perspective described by
Silverman (1970), is that it focuses on the immediate social
and informational context within which behaviour occurs.
Rather than seeing needs as inherent properties of the person,

they are personally or socially ascribed in order to explain behaviour. Thus, while need satisfaction models (Maslow 1943; Alderfer 1972) regard individual attributes and job characteristics as the important element in predicting job attitudes, the social information processing perspective shifts attention to the array of social influences and consequences of past choices as the determinants of attitudes.

Salancik and Pfeffer detail three such causes of attitude or need statements. One refers to the effect of an individual's past behaviours and how these behaviours come to be attributed to the individual or the environment; and much of the literature reviewed above in the sections on commitment and insufficient justification is cited to support this point. The other two refer to the way the individual perceives the affective components of his job and work situation, and how he chooses to interpret salient social cues. His cognitive evaluation of this environment does not rely on objectively given job features but draws upon information about his own past expression of attitudes, others' expression of attitudes, and the behavioural responses of himself and others. In other words, though the experience is immediate, perception is a retrospective process, depending on recall, which because it is incomplete will result in an environment, or reality, which is in fact constructed through individual and social processes (Berger and Luckman 1967; Weick 1969).

What relevance does this model have to graduate job choice? Before choosing a job, students develop expectations about a number of job alternatives from many informational sources. Inevitably, this information will be less than comprehensive, and anyway some aspects will not be remembered. Hence, the final picture of what it is like to work for a particular company is partly based on objective data but is largely reconstructed. Once employed, the social context, comprising fellow graduates, older colleagues, family and friends, will continue to affect attitudes, together with the many socially-mediated implications of the job choice itself; these might include the graduate's commitment to his choice, the information about job choice that happens to be salient at the time the attitude is generated, and the social norms and expectations governing what constitutes a rational explanation for his original choice.

AUTONOMY OF JOB CHOICE

In this chapter the various areas of literature pertaining to organizational choice have been reviewed, with the purpose of determining which - if any - aspects of this choice process affect the entrant's initial satisfaction with, and commitment to the chosen employer.

Two contrasting theoretical frameworks have been addressed, both of which attribute explanatory value to choice variables. On the one hand mainstream research takes an implicity hedonistic view of motivation, such that choice is made on the basis of a rational assessment of job alternatives and personal work goals as posited by expectancy theorists (Vroom 1964; Porter and Lawler 1968): positive job attitudes are directly dependent on extrinsic rewards, as predicated by the inducements, contributions model (March and Simon 1958), and upon the match between personal needs and the objective characteristics of the job and organization, as implied by various versions of the needs-satisfaction model (Maslow 1943; Alderfer 1972; Hackman and Lawler 1971) as well as being integral to the met expectations hypothesis (Wanous 1977; Louis 1980). Finally this prospectively rational line of argument extends to the prediction that, when alternative opportunities for employment are available to the employee, job dissatisfaction will increase and lead to voluntary turnover (Price 1977; Muchinsky and Tuttle 1979). Applying these theoretical predictions to graduate job entry, it would be expected that students, given a fairly informed job choice together with reasonable extrinsic rewards once with the company, would be satisfied and committed employees. This is based on the straightforward model that work attitudes and behaviour are a function of met expectations and of the objective characteristics of the organization, job and job incumbent.

On the other hand an increasing number of researchers reviewed in the latter part of this chapter have examined some of the implications of choice, particularly if the outcome transpires to be negative, which the earlier analysis of graduate follow-up studies invariably revealed (Dunette et al 1973; Bray et al 1974; Parsons and Hutt 1981). If, indeed, unfavourable consequences are perceived to ensue, the individual is predicted to follow one of a number of retrospective strategies to minimise the dissonance caused by what seems to be behavioural or decisional error (Staw 1980). This thinking stems originally from Festinger's (1957) dissonance theory which posited that any two cognitive elements, such as beliefs or opinions, about oneself or the environment, which are inconsistent with each other lead to a psychologically uncomfortable state of cognitive dissonance; which, in turn, leads to rationalisation in the form of attitude change. Further elements have been built upon this foundational theory which refine and elaborate its predictive power, and increase its applicability to organizational choice. It has been argued, for example, that commitment, in the form of freedom and irrevocability of original choice, serves to enhance the effects of dissonance (Kiesler and Sakamura 1966; Salancik 1977); furthermore, according to the insufficient justification hypothesis (Pfeffer and Lawler 1980), where there is such prior commitment, then ironically when extrinsic rewards are made salient attitudes become less favourable.

Thus, in contrast to the predictions of the prospective model above, it is stated that attitudes or 'need statements' (Salancik and Pfeffer 1978) are derived from prior behaviour and actions, rather than behaviour flowing from pre-formed attitudes. Secondly, many of the postulates of this retrospective approach involve the counterhedonic influence of extrinsic motivations or rewards on attitudes. An analysis of graduate job choice and transition into work would therefore have to carefully consider the circumstantial context of the decision, in particular the extent to which job choice was externally constrained or autonomously chosen.

What this review has shown then, is that there are several features of the job choice process, apart from the job and organizational expectations explored in the previous chapter, which are salient to the development of future work attitudes. Research reflecting the prospective orientation tends to reinforce the findings of the expectations' studies : that a person's needs and work-goals, together with the extent of his previous work experience which is a major influence in identifying needs and shaping goals, are important factors in subsequent job satisfaction.

The other two elements of the job choice process that this prospective focus highlights are the perceived opportunities available to the decision-maker and the influence of significant others in assessing those alternatives and making the final choice. As it happens, the retrospective approach, focusing, as it does, on some of the psychological ramifications of choice, also reveals that external constraints are a crucial - indeed could be determining - factor in the formation of future work attitudes.

Given the disproportionately high turnover of graduates from their first employers discovered in the review of follow-up studies, chapters two and three have been devoted to analysing the possible antecedents to this phenomenum. As noted by Wanous (1977) the field of job entry has been addressed from three primary perspectives. Research has tended to view this process from an organizational orientation rather than the individual's viewpoint (for example Dunette 1966), or alternatively, to concentrate on occupational, rather than organizational, choice and entry, or finally, to describe and relate job attitudes to aspects of socialisation once the employee is _inside_ the organization (for example, Schein 1968). Between these well researched areas there remains the relatively uncharted field of job entry from the individual's viewpoint and how _pre_-entry variables affect his subsequent work attitudes.

Thus, the preceding literature review has drawn upon diverse streams of research, each of which partially bridges this gap. The process of graduate job entry has been viewed from three angles : first the expectations literature which until recently predominated discussion of job attitudes amongst new employees; second, the conventional approach to organizational choice which also adopts a prospective view of decision-making and job-individual matching; third a relatively recent body of literature which has applied dissonance theory and various related retrospective paradigms to choosing jobs. From these reviews a number of vital variables have been isolated for inclusion in this research project. Under what circumstances they will exert influence, to what extent they are complementary, especially considering the opposite predictions of some prospective and retrospective theories, and what precise effects they can be expected to have upon dependent variables are all, as yet, unanswered questions. The following chapter which develops a research model and hypotheses will seek to address and resolve these issues.

NOTES

(1) The word rational requires some explanation, since in a totally subjective sense any behaviour could be described as rational. However, following Staw (1980), rationality here is viewed as 'decision-making approximating economic utility theory or expectancy theories of behaviour' (p.57); according to this definition the individual processes information and makes a decision to attain a high level of outcomes, as against a situation where he re-evaluates alternatives and outcomes to make it appear that he has acted in a competent manner, to himself and/or other people. The latter self justifying behaviour could be termed rationalisation.

4 Model and methods

So far it has been concluded that newcomers' expectations are a crucial factor in their satisfaction and desire to stay with the company they had chosen to join. Less emphatic and empirically consistent are the explanations as to why this relationship should occur. However, researchers typically build upon a model of matching individual needs and abilities with organizational opportunities and requirements. The central postulation is that where expectations are realistic and/or subsequently fulfilled a good match has been achieved, leading to positive attitudes and organizational commitment; negative outcomes follow a poor match.

The research on job choice dealt with in chapter three draws together a less straightforward series of theoretical frameworks. Nevertheless, the unifying thread from the various paradigms and theories reviewed is the tendency for attitudes to be retrospectively adjusted to bring them into alignment with previous actions and their outcomes, in this case, the decision of a graduate to work with a particular company. On the face of it, the two basic models underlying the discussion in chapters two and three seem to be fundamentally incompatible. However, closer scrutiny reveals that both have distinctive value in helping interpret and explain the transition to work process.

The expectations thesis is the key to understanding job attitudes in the more ideal situation where a graduate selects rationally from a number of job offers; when the circumstances surrounding his initial decision are constraining and/or the consequences of the choice prove to be negative, then the job choice model, in its various components, is indispensible to unravel the more intricate retrospective processes that ensue. Hence, far from being mutually exclusive, an analysis of the early satisfaction and commitment of graduates that is dependent on one or other of these models would be inadequate. Yet, to the author's knowledge, no previous study of this area has deliberately incorporated expectations and job choice as complementary, independent variables (1).

This chapter will examine the construction of the above two models in turn, applying them to the graduate job entry context. Then a summary model will be proposed which synthesises the two and embraces the major control variables identified elsewhere. Arising from this overall model the hypotheses will be stated, and the final section on methods will describe how they are to be tested.

THE EFFECTS OF REALISTIC EXPECTATIONS

Although many authors have implicitly adopted the matching model as a theoretical framework, it is Wanous who has attempted to depict it graphically (Wanous 1978; 1980).

Because much of the research on realistic expectations is based on experiments with realistic job previews (RJPs), administered by various means to incoming employees prior to their joining the organization, Wanous takes the RJP as the starting point for his model. Evidence for the relationship between the RJP and job tenure is fairly strong: all six experiments testing this link, reviewed by Wanous (1977) showed greater job survival rates for those employees who had received realistic job previews, although the differences from the control group were not always statistically significant and in some cases the sample studies had only been with the company for four weeks (the maximum in other studies was one year after entry), which is perhaps too soon to assess turnover effects.

It can be seen from the unrealistic expectations model in figure 4.1 that between the RJP and job satisfaction are a series of intervening linkages which seek to explain and elaborate this relationship. The empirical bases for these have already been reviewed in chapter two. Evidence for the link between RJP and vaccination of initial expectations was demonstrated in the two studies which examined this (Wanous

1977; Youngberg 1963), but Wanous admits (1978) that the other hypothesised linkages remain, as yet, speculative; a view confirmed by Louis (1980) and recently borne out by Dugoni and Ilgen (1981) in a systematic testing of them. With regard to the commitment link, research from the field of decision-making and choice (for instance, Bem 1970; Lepper and Greene 1975; O'Reilly and Caldwell 1980) would certainly support the notion that freedom from coercion and/or participation in the decision leads to greater internal commitment to the choice or 'locus of control', which in turn enhances satisfaction; but it is not clear why vaccination of expectations should cause this, since the important factor here is <u>perception</u> of choice, rather than reality. It is possible that a person could freely select an organization from several alternatives and therefore feel commited to the choice and subsequently satisfied, despite the fact that the decision was based unwittingly on unrealistic job information.

When the above points have been taken into account, together with the problems of using RJPs to operationalise the realistic expectations variable, we find the Wanous' model adds little to the previous matching models which posit that a needs-climates match leads to increased satisfaction and commitment, and lower turnover. However, the other branch of expectations literature, dealing with unmet expectations, provides a more substantial initial relationship between realistic expectations and the matching process. The two branches are compared in figure 4.1 introducing an organizational entry time boundary. As found by Ward and Athos (1972), Bray, Campbell and Grant (1974) and Wanous (1976), the pre-entry expectations of employees, especially graduates, are typically inflated. The subsequent job satisfaction, performance and tenure of newcomers is directly related to the degree to which expectations concerning the job and organization are, or are not, fulfilled, because they experience more or less of desired aspects than anticipated (Katzell 1968; Dunette, Arvey and Banas 1973; Kotter 1973; Morse 1975; Schneider 1975a). In the unrealistic expectations model it is the original, pre-entry level of expectations that are hypothesised to have significant effects on future satisfaction and commitment. Whereas in the unmet expectations model realism of expectations is still the crucial element; this time it is compared to actual post-entry experience and the <u>discrepancy</u> is related to job attitudes and behaviour.

Louis (1980) points out that findings from the literature on product performance ratings, citing Oliver (1977), document independent and separate effects of first initial expectations and second, disconfirmed expectations. Thus, despite the

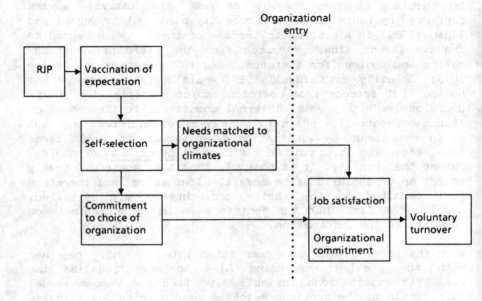

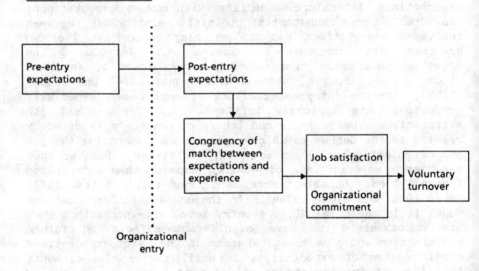

Figure 4.1 A comparison of the unrealistic and the unmet expectations models

58

weightier empirical support for the influence of unmet
expectations on job attitudes, both hypotheses will be tested
here in order to unravel their respective and differential
impact.

THE EFFECTS OF JOB CHOICE AUTONOMY

We have already noted that level of expectations alone cannot
adequately explain an individual's satisfaction and commitment
(2). This is primarily because the expectations model assumes
job candidates behave in a wholly prospective and rational
manner whereas research has shown that although this may be
partially true, choosing an organization is likely to bring
into play various retrospective strategies which can have
significant influences on a new employee's statement of
satisfaction and desire to stay with the organization.

For instance the effects of cognitive dissonance will
influence the graduate who is choosing jobs in the following
way. If there are no or few alternatives the decision to join
an organization is involuntary, or at least, highly
constrained, which itself provides justification for the act:
so an individual can explain his dissatisfaction in terms of
poor choice of viable job options. In contrast, where an
individual is faced with several viable alternatives in the
job choice context dissonance is aroused because his decision
to select one option and reject a number of others suggests
inconsistency which itself requires internal justification
(presumably, this would not occur if all but one of the given
alternatives were palpably unacceptable). However,
longitudinal follow-up studies of graduate entrants (Vroom and
Deci 1971; Lawler, Kuleck, Rhode and Sorenson 1975) have found
this phenomenon to be short-lived, which is where the concept
of commitment becomes important.

The literature on commitment (Kiesler and Sakamura 1966;
Kiesler 1971; Salancik 1977) demonstrates that the very act of
choice, especially if it is autonomous, explicit and
irrevocable, is a powerful constraint on future behaviour and
introduces another retrospective mechanism: that of attitude
reconstruction. If the job choice transpires to have negative
consequences and the original decision was made free from
external constraints then the concept of commitment binds the
individual to bring his attitudes into line with his initial
action. This serves to prove to himself (3) that he did not
make a mistake in committing himself to an unattractive job
(Festinger and Carlsmith 1957; Pallak, Sogin and Van Zante
1974; Staw 1980). A variation on this rationalising mechanism

is for the individual to attempt to recoup his losses by actually escalating his commitment to the course of action, which has hitherto had negative outcomes, since resisting change is another feature of commitment theory (Kiesler and Sakamura 1966; Staw and Fox 1977). A further strategy individuals can adopt to rationalise their action is to search for what Staw (1980) calls exogenerating explanations: that is, to look for external factors beyond his control either in the job situation, the outcome, or in the circumstances surrounding the original job choice which can be blamed for the negative consequences. Whatever the route chosen to alleviate the inconsistency, the vital catalyst is that the individual freely chose the organization and feels personally responsible for that decision since it is these aspects which induce the binding effect of commitment.

Research findings from the field of insufficient justification add further ramifications to organizational choice, with the adoption of similar retrospective strategies. The basic model of the effects of insufficient justification predicts that both extrinsic rewards, and commitment will have direct positive influences on job attitudes: this is only what we might expect according to need-satisfaction and commitment theories respectively, as discussed above. But, ironically, there is also a posited indirect effect of extrinsic rewards on attitudes as follows: intrinsic rewards are taken to be causally, negatively related to the presence and magnitude of extrinsic rewards and to extrinsic rewards interacting with commitment. This leads to the prediction that when extrinsic rewards are greater the intrinsic rewards for staying with the organization are smaller, and this relationship will be accentuated by the presence of commitment (Pfeffer and Lawler 1980). Thus, in short, individuals who have either joined the organization for intrinsic reasons or who are presently experiencing intrinsic rewards (4) will, in the absence of extrinsic motivations, retrospectively develop their own justification for their action, leading to a positive effect on their attitudes, (this runs counter to the rational model which would hypothesise negative job attitude resulting from the absence of extrinsic rewards).

At this point it may be helpful to draw together the various threads of the retrospective focus into a summary model. It has been noted that whether the theoretical framework is that of dissonance, commitment or insufficient justification, the degree of autonomy exercised by an individual in his original job choice is the key factor in retrospective rationalisation: in other words, the circumstances under which the graduate makes his job choice may come to have a primary influence on his satisfaction with and commitment to that company.

An elaboration of the kind of factors which determine freedom of choice is made by Salancik (1977). Following Kiesler and Sakamura (1966), he specifies four characteristics of behavioural acts which make them binding, and consequently serve to enhance future commitment. These are explicitness, revocability, publicity and volition. He further identifies four dimensions of perceived volition: first, the degree to which choice is autonomously exercised; second, the presence of external demands for action; third, the presence of other extrinsic, as against intrinsic, bases for action; and fourth, the presence of other contributors to action. O'Reilly and Caldwell (1981) empirically tested these propositions in a longitudinal study of graduates and found that those who had made their original job choice volitionally and perceived their decision to be irrevocable, were more satisfied and committed six months later. But no such relationship was found for the explictness and publicity variables.

It is clear, then, that the retrospective focus may well incorporate reference back to at least some of the constraining pressures present at the time of the original job choice, as well as to aspects of job choice and outcome. Figure 4.2 summarises some of the effects of autonomy of job choice on job satisfaction and commitment.

A SYNTHESIS OF MODELS

Having discussed the main variables arising from the expectations model (figure 4.1) and highlighted the pertinent variables emerging from the retrospective focus (figure 4.2), we can now proceed to combine the two models into one total model depicting the effect of expectations and autonomy of choice on job satisfaction and organizational commitment (figure 4.3).

The fact that these two theoretical frameworks have not previously been incorporated in this way suggests a serious weakness of research in this field, resulting in a hitherto incomplete treatment of the effects of pre-entry variables on subsequent job attitudes and behaviour. Surely individuals act neither in a wholly rational, nor entirely in a self-justifying manner; and this composite model attempts to reflect at a theoretical level the range of both prospective and retrospective possibilities surrounding the job choice process and trace their differential impact on job satisfaction and organization commitment.

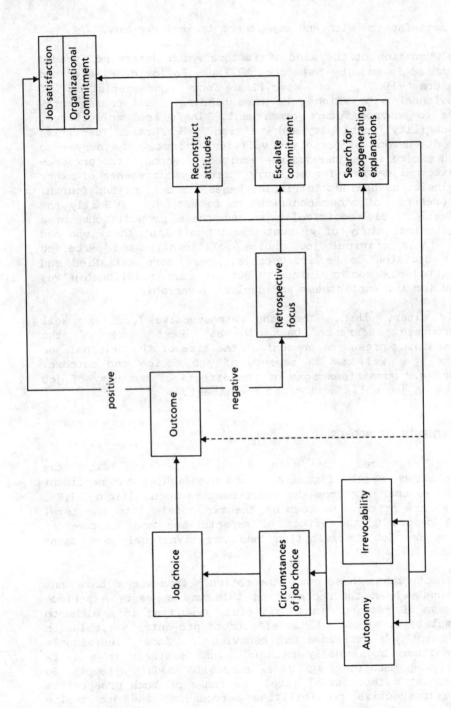

Figure 4.2   The effects of autonomy of choice on job satisfaction and commitment

Thus, it can be seen that the effects predicted by the expectations hypotheses rest upon a prospective premise: the individual compares his experience of his chosen job and organization with what he anticipates prior to joining. The match or mis-match between the two, assessed in terms of either pre-entry realism or pre-entry/post-entry congruency, is registered as job satisfaction and organizational commitment.

The effect of autonomy of choice on these same dependent variables rests upon a similarly prospective and rational perspective. However, the circumstances of job choice and entry are frequently less than ideal: on the one hand, the actual decision to accept a company offer may be perceived as irrevocable and/or constrained by one of a number of external influences, not least the increasing competitiveness of the graduate labour market; on the other hand, the experienced outcome of that choice, even when made relatively autonomously is often disappointing. When this is the case, or when there is a lack of extrinsic rewards accruing to organizational membership, the behaviour and attitudes of new employees are no longer explicable simply in terms of a match between the individual needs, aspirations and expectations and organizational requirements, climates and opportunities. An analysis which takes account of retrospective processes, together with their appropriate self-justifying strategies, now becomes crucial.

Depending on which strategy is adopted, they either loop back to the choice, where circumstances surrounding the original decision are singled out as 'excuses', or to the outcome stage of the model whereby consequences of the choice are re-evaluated or alternatively related directly to job satisfaction and organizational commitment via irrational escalation of commitment or reconstructed attitudes. Although these mechanisms of rationalisation have been briefly discussed earlier, it is beyond our scope here to actually test them independently and so in this summary model they are corporately labelled retrospective strategies.

In addition to the primary relationships between independent and dependent variables, a number of background variables have been included in the model, dividing into three broad categories: biographical factors, educational factors and work-related factors. To avoid unnecessary confusion of the model, only some of the more obvious of these projected relationships are indicated by broken lines.

On the basis of this model (figure 4.3) it can be hypothesised

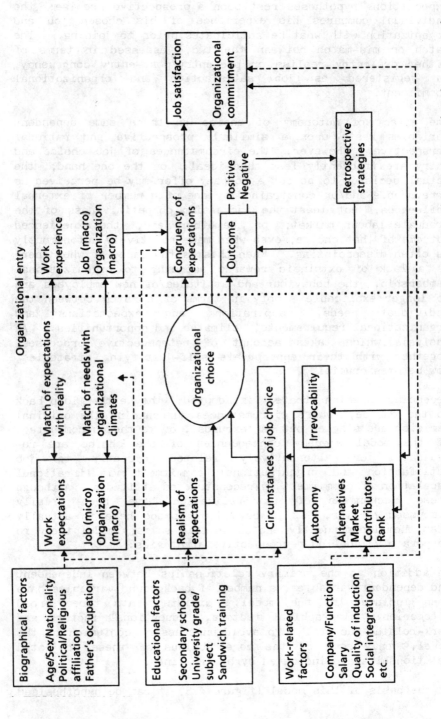

Figure 4.3 The effect of expectations and job choice on job satisfaction and organizational commitment

that the job satisfaction and organizational commitment expressed by graduate entrants will be influenced by the following factors:

1. The degree to which there is congruency between pre-entry expectations concerning a number of job features, and the actual experience of those features six months after entry.
2. The level of pre-entry expectations concerning the chosen job and organization.

3. The number of suitable alternatives available at the time of job choice.

4. The perceived freedom from labour market constraints at the time of job choice.

5. The perceived freedom from other contributors to the job choice decision.

6. The rank of the chosen job according to the graduate's original personal preference.

7. The irrevocability of the job choice, as perceived prior to entry.

METHOD

In order to test these hypotheses a survey was conducted with the graduate intake of 20 companies in the UK engineering sector. Two weeks prior to commencing employment a total of 354 graduates received questionnaires at their homes; 214 were returned, representing a response rate of 69 per cent. Approximately six months later the new addresses of these 214 were secured from their respective employers and a second stage questionnaire was posted to them. (It was felt important that respondents should complete the questionnaire in an out-of-work setting to obtain a more reflective response, to avoid collaboration between subjects, and to reinforce the independent nature of the research in which replies would be treated with strict confidentiality). 134 of these completed and returned a second stage questionnaire, comprising of 64 per cent response rate, or 42 per cent overall. Naturally, there was an element of self-selective bias in both first and second stage responses; however, there was no marked difference on a number of key variables when the residual sample was compared firstly with the national cohort from which it was drawn (Universities' Statistics Record 1982), and secondly, with the non-respondents to the second questionnaire.

The sample comprised university graduates primarily from engineering and technology courses (71 per cent) and constituted 2.3 per cent of the national cohort entering the industrial employment sectors. They divided almost equally between sandwich training and full-time students, and their employers ranged from two large public companies to a number of smaller private manufacturing organizations. In the interim between stages one and two, only two of the sample had changed employer, although it is probable that a number of those not responding to the second questionnaire had left their first companies.

Variables measured

The need to distinguish between the separately significant effects of initial and disconfirmed expectations has been made by Louis (1980). It was for this reason that the research design adopted here took independent measurements of pre-entry level and post-entry congruency of expectations. The first stage questionnaire contained a list of 20 statements concerning the macro and micro climates of the organization, compiled from expectations inventories used by Kotter (1972) and Dunette et al (1973), and from a pilot survey using open-ended interviews with British graduates (5). This index was repeated at stage two. In each case respondents were asked to rate the accuracy of each statement according to the knowledge they had at the time on a five point scale.

Post entry congruency   Three measures of congruency were derived from a comparison of these two descriptive ratings: match, the number of exactly corresponding scores; mismatch, a summation of the total difference between the two indices; and weighted discrepancy, a score of the difference which also accounted for the relative importance of job features recorded by subjects elsewhere on both the first and second stage questionnaires.

Pre-entry level was assessed by taking one mean socre from the pre-entry expectations over the same 20 items. Preliminary analysis showed that two control variables also provided a valid indication of pre-entry level: these were the amount of time spent working previously in a relevant industry or with the company that was subsequently joined.

Arising from the theoretical work of Kiesler and Sakamura (1966) and Kiesler (1971), Salancik in 1977 specified several conditions under which choice was likely to be particularly binding, and it is these criteria which O'Reilly and Caldwell test in their longitudinal study of MBA graduates (1980; 1981). By adapting the questions asked in this latter study to make them more pertinent to the UK context, the following aspects of autonomy were tapped at stage one.

Revocability concerns the extent to which a decision is reversible. In fact few actions are really reversible, but some have more permanent implications and can only be undone with great difficulty; the more the individual perceives this to be the case the more binding the original action is. This variable was assessed by asking respondents at time one how difficult it would be to change jobs within the next year if they so desired. Although this is especially salient before entry because of its temporal proximity to the original job choice, an identical question was asked at time two to see if this perception had changed over the transition period.

To ascertain freedom of choice, respondents were asked 'how many suitable alternatives did you have to choose from when you accepted the job?' A high number here constitutes greater freedom of choice, and a low number or none constituting low choice.

The presence of external demands for action refers to the circumstantial constraints exerted on the individual from sources beyond his control. It was felt that a question concerning the constraints of the graduate labour market encapsulated well this dimension for a UK job seeker and this was consequently embedded in a list of five factors which respondents were asked to rate as to its importance in influencing their decision to accept the job. A high score here indicates that the competitiveness of the graduate labour market was a very important consideration in the decision; in other words there were high external demands for action and autonomy of choice was low.

The third dimension of volition is the existence of extrinsic bases for action, and this was operationalised by asking subjects : ' According to your original preference, where does the job you have accepted rank among the total number applied for?' By indicating whether the job is first, second or fifth, or lower, the respondent is revealing in quantifiable terms his preference for the job compared with other alternatives, which may or may not have materialised. Obtaining a job of high rank equates with low extrinsic basis for action and therefore high freedom of choice, whereas taking a job low in preference demonstrates an extrinsically based decision with concomitant low choice.

To examine the presence of other <u>contributors to action</u> subjects were asked to rate on a five point scale : 'To what extent do you feel you were influenced by others (eg. family, friends) in your choice of job?' In this case a high score indicates that the presence of other contributors was influential in the decision, with a correspondingly low freedom of choice; in contrast a low score signifies higher personal responsibility and freedom of choice.

<u>Job satisfaction</u> was evaluated at stage two by asking the respondent to rate general satisfaction and preference to move to another job (both 5-point scales), and also by a 10 item index. These items were devised specifically for this research from two sources: previous studies of UK graduates by Hill (1969) and Mansfield (1971), and the open-ended pilot interviews. The total of scores for each of the 10 items provided an overall satisfaction measure; also each item was weighted according to its equivalent ranking on the job importance index, this was felt to comprise a very sensitive measure of the individual's subjective evaluation of the job.

<u>Organizational commitment.</u> Consistent with previous use (Mowday et al 1979; Angle and Perry 1981), the Organizational Commitment Questionnaire (OCQ) was scored by averaging the individual scores, ranging from one to seven, across the 15 items. The two subscales of this, values commitment and commitment to stay were also computed. In addition, following O'Reilly and Caldwell (1981), separate measures were made of plans to remain with the company, answered on a five point scale of certainty, and future tenure intention, measured in terms of years.

<u>Control variables.</u> In order to assess the impact of more objective differences in individuals, organizations and jobs upon the dependent variables, biographical details, education and training information as well as work-related data were also collected.

<u>Open-ended questions.</u> In his picture of what a newcomer is likely to experience Louis (1980) distinguishes three conceptual categories to help understand the entry process : change, contrast and surprise which precede sense-making where the individual successfully or unsuccessfully adapts to organizational life. Change refers to external, objective differences like location, job function and salary. Surprise embraces the differences between the new entrant's anticipation and actual experience in the organization, and this area is tapped by the expectations inventory. However the middle element of contrast which refers to those

differences that emerge in the newcomer's perceptual field as personally significant and uniquely experienced characteristics of the new situation can only be captured by an open-ended response format. At the end of the second questionnaire, therefore, three questions were asked which give respondents the opportunity to expand on responses previously intimated in the fixed choice sections, or to introduce entirely new aspects which could not have been anticipated by the researcher, or even by the subject, but have emerged to have special significance. This data is recorded in chapter eight.

NOTES.

(1)   Even the longitudinal study of graduates by O'Reilly and Caldwell (1981), which acknowledges the mutual efficacy of both models, only tested job choice variables as independent; expectations was held constant as a control variable.

(2)   For instance, Salancik and Pfeffer (1977 p.453) conclude that studies based on the need-satisfaction model almost never explain more than 40% of variance in job satisfaction, leaving a tremendous amount of variance unaccounted for.

(3)   The concept of 'proving himself right' is for the actor's own benefit, not for the sake of appearing consistent before onlookers. The latter may happen, but striving for this public consistency would not, by itself, bring about the kind of true change in the individual's attitudes that the commitment model posits.

(4)   For two cognitions to be psychologically inconsistent it is not necessary that they be logically inconsistent. In this example, it is not unreasonable for an individual to be working at a job with low extrinsic rewards, people often work for little or no rewards, but it is psychologically inconsistent and hence the motivation to rationalise the inconsistency is engendered.

(5)   Using a very simple interview schedule 12 unstructured interviews were conducted in June 1981 with graduating students to solicit the kind of expectations and job needs they had as they prepared for full-time employement. These graduates were from Reading and Brunel Universities and comprised both sandwich and full-time students so as to reflect any differences in work attitudes that may have evolved from their varying familiarity with industry. Notes taken from these interviews were then used in the compilation of the expectations and job needs' inventories.

5 Company comparison

In this chapter the mean values of a number of key variables will be discussed using the organization as the unit of analysis. Apart from providing a useful descriptive summary of the frequencies data this approach also yields informative patterns and relationships between variables which is then subsequently pursued with more rigorous correlative techniques at an individual level of analysis.

Since the final sample size of some of the organizations was too small for meaningful statistical analysis, those with nine or less respondents were grouped according to their employment sector.   This yielded an adjusted list of participating companies as given in table 5.1.

Initially the data has been arranged according to company categories (table 5.2);   from this intercompany differences, previously concealed within the statistics for the total sample,   become readily apparent.   This is refined in table 5.3, by breaking down company subsamples into their sandwich and non-sandwich trained graduates.   Part of the research design was to aim for an even distribution of sandwich and non-sandwich students across the sample since it was felt that this might prove to be an important contributory factor in the formation of realistic work expectations.   The base figures in table 5.3 show that these subsamples were achieved for each of the companies,   though in some cases the numbers are rather small.   The findings of these tables will be reviewed under

TABLE 5.1 - A breakdown of response rates by adjusted company categories

COMPANY	LABEL	PRINCIPAL ACTIVITY	QUESTIONNAIRE 1				QUESTIONNAIRE 2		OVERALL % RESPONSE
			NO SENT	NO RETURNED	LATE OR SPOILT	% RESPONSE	NO RETURNED	% RESPONSE	
British Rail	BR	PUBLIC MANUFACTURING	57	38	3	72.0	25	66.0	43.9
G.E.C.	GEC	PRIVATE MANUFACTURING	52	27	1	53.8	17	63.0	33.0
BRITISH GAS	BGAS	PUBLIC UTILITIES	33	22	2	72.7	12	54.5	36.4
B.P.	BP	PRIVATE OIL/CHEMICAL	31	18	2	64.5	12	66.7	38.7
KELLOGG	KELL	CONSTRUCTION	14	12	1	92.8	10	83.3	71.4
BABCOCK etc (a)	MAN	OTHER MANUFACTURING	127	69	3	56.7	44	63.7	34.6
LAING etc (b)	MANCON	MANUFACTURING/ CONSTRUCTION	40	28	2	75.0	14	50.5	35.0
			354	214	14	69.6	134	64.0	41.8

a) This category also includes : Metal Box, Ford, Rolls Royce, Tube Investments, Marconi Space & Defence, Reed International, ICI (Paints), Plessey, Ferranti, and Foster Wheeler.

b) This category also includes : Bechtel and John Brown.

TABLE 5.2 - Mean values of selected variables by company category

VARIABLE	BR(25)	GEC(17)	BGAS(12)	BP(12)	KELL(10)	MAN(45)	MANCON(14)	TOTAL SAMPLE
JOB CHOICE								
Alternatives	1.6	1.5	1.4	2.7	1.3	1.8	1.3	1.7
Market Pressure	2.5	2.5	2.8	2.3	2.4	2.4	3.6 $t = 3.14^{\circ\circ\circ}$	2.6
External Constraints	4.0	3.7	4.0	4.0	4.4	4.2	3.6	4.0
Rank Preference	1.5	1.5	1.9	1.7	2.0	2.2	2.1	1.8
EXPECTATIONS								
Pre-entry level	73.3	65.6 $t = 4.43^{\circ\circ\circ}$	70.6	79.1 $t = 3.75^{\circ\circ\circ}$	71.2	72.5	74.1	72.3
Discrepancy	33.4	16.0 $t = 1.87^{*}$	36.8	19.0	73.1 $t = 2.00^{\circ}$	29.0	24.3	30.8
Job Satisfaction	191.4	189.7	171.9	198.5 $t = 2.67^{\circ\circ}$	149.6 $t = 6.33^{\circ\circ\circ}$	190.6	186.6	186.1
Commitment	54.0	45.7	47.1	56.6 $t = 2.74^{\circ\circ}$	46.5	53.5	54.9	51.9

$^{*}p < .10$; $^{\circ}p < .05$; $^{\circ\circ}p < .02$; $^{\circ\circ\circ}p < .01$

TABLE 5.2 CONT'D

VARIABLE	BR(25)	GEC(17)	BGAS(12)	BP(12)	KELL(10)	MAN(45)	MANCON(14)	TOTAL SAMPLE
CONTROL								
Progress Towards Placement	3.7	3.7	2.9 $t = 1.73^{•}$	3.6	3.0	3.9	3.6	3.6
Social Integration	2.0 $t = 3.35^{ooo}$	3.0	2.3	3.0	3.0	3.3	2.6	2.8
Quality of Training	3.6	3.3	3.3	3.3	1.8 $t = 3.91^{ooo}$	3.7	3.2	3.4
Performance Feedback	4.0	3.5	4.3 $t = 5.53^{ooo}$	1.6 $t = 6.66^{ooo}$	4.5 $t = 7.19^{ooo}$	3.3	2.1 $t = 4.18^{ooo}$	3.4
Salary Level	2.5	2.1	2.3	3.5 $t = 4.71^{ooo}$	3.1 $t = 4.06^{ooo}$	2.3	2.6	2.5

•P<.10; °P<.05; °°P<.02; °°°P<.01

73

four headings : first, looking at those variables relating to the two independent variables, job choice and expectations; third, at some of the more salient control variables; and finally at the dependent variables, job satisfaction and organizational commitment.

DESCRIPTION OF RESULTS BY COMPANY

Job Choice variables

It can be seen that graduates from BP had more alternatives to choose from when applying for their jobs than their counterparts in other companies, and this is particularly true of their sandwich students (t= 2.52, p <10). It seems that being destined for BP did not diminish the perception that they had a number of other viable job options open to them. In contrast the sandwich students from other companies were consistently more pessimistic about the number of other job offers than their non-sandwich colleagues in the same organizations; indeed the three sandwich graduates at KELL perceived no alternatives at all when taking up employment (1). BP graduates also felt less constrained by the labour market when making their job choice, though this variance with other companies is not significant. On the other hand those starting with MANCON were significantly more pressurised by this factor, especially sandwich graduates, presumably because these companies were in a more highly competitive employment situation at the time.

Generally the influence of others on the decision was perceived to be low by all respondents with an overall mean score of four on a scale of five. However the more detailed breakdown of Table 5.3 reveals that GEC sandwich and MANCON non-sandwich graduates register significantly greater constraint on this facet of job choice. As far as rank preference scores, the means for companies cluster around the overall mean of 1.8, where one is equivalent to first choice, two to second choice and so on; but significant variance from this again shows up on table 5.3 where BP and KELL sandwich graduates (t=3.80, p <.01) both achieved job offers closest to their original preference. It is probable that a large proportion had either worked for, and/or were sponsored by these organizations as students, hence their preference as first choice was virtually predetermined. In contrast KELL non-sandwich graduates had the lowest mean score for this variable; in other words the chosen company conformed to their original personal preference least often.

TABLE 5.3 - Mean values of selected variables by company and sandwich training

VARIABLE	BR N/S	S	GEC N/S	S	BGAS N/S	S	BP N/S	S	KELL N/S	S	MAN N/S	S	MANCON N/S	S	TOTAL SAMPLE N/S	S
JOB CHOICE																
alternative	1.6	1.6	1.9	1.0	2.0	0.8	2.6	2.8 (t=2.52*)	1.9	.0 (t=7.75°°°)	1.8	1.8	1.3	1.3	1.8	1.4
market pressure	2.9	2.0	2.4	2.5	3.2	2.5	2.4	2.0	2.4	2.0	2.3	2.7	3.2	4.0 (t=3.65°°°)	2.6	2.6
external constraints	4.1	3.9	4.0	3.3 (t=1.85*)	3.7	4.3	4.1	3.8	4.3	4.7	4.3	4.1	3.2	4.0 (t=1.80*)	4.1	3.9
rank preference	1.6	1.5	1.5	1.5	2.0	1.8	2.0	1.0 (t=3.80°°°)	2.5	1.80 (t=3.80°°°)	2.2	2.3	2.3	2.0	1.9	1.7
EXPECTATIONS																
pre-entry level	76.9	69.1	65.3	65.8 (t=4.52°°°)	72.4	69.2	77.6	82.0 (t=4.06°°°)	75.7	60.7	72.1	73.5	76.7	72.1	73.3	70.6
discrepancy	38.2	28.0	22.1	9.1	38.7	34.8	21.9	13.3 (t=1.85*)	100.0	10.3 (t=3.85°°°)	29.9	26.9	11.5	33.9 (t=2.06°)	34.9	24.5
job satisfaction	201.8	180.4	186.8	193.0	189.3	154.5	202.1	191.5 (t=1.98°)	149.7	149.3 (t=1.98° t=1.73*)	190.5	190.8	199.2	177.3	189.9	180.3
commitment	57.4	50.3	46.7	44.5	47.5	46.7	56.5	56.8 (t=1.85*)	46.7	46.0	54.5	50.9	60.7	50.5 (t=2.91°°)	53.6	49.4

*P<.10; °P<.05; °°P<.02; °°°P<.01   N/S Non-sandwich, S sandwich

75

Expectations variables

The two elements of expectations examined here are level of pre-entry expectations and weighted discrepancy between expectations and actual experience. It might reasonably be predicted from the expectations literature that the mean values for these two variables would be positively related for each company : if the level of expectations prior to starting work with an organization is high, then it is more likely that the ensuing discrepancy will also be high, since graduates invariably have an inflated picture of what their jobs are going to be like. The intercompany comparison shows this to be the case for only one company : in GEC the level of expectations is significantly lower than the overall mean, a finding which can be attributed primarily to the non-sandwich graduates whose work expectations were unusually deflated ($t=4.52$, $p < .001$) compared to non-sandwich entrants to other companies.   After several months at work the incongruence between these relatively low expectations and their experience was significantly low ($t=1.87$, $p < .10$). However BP graduates registered very high expectations at the pre-entry stage ($t=3.75$, $p < .001$) yet the mean for weighted discrepancy was comparatively low, especially for non-sandwich employees ($t=3.85$, $p < .001$), the group that would be anticipated to encounter the greatest disenchantment.   Also the mean score for discrepancy for KELL graduates was significantly high, particularly for their non-sandwich entrants ($t=3.85$, $p < .001$) but the high means for pre-entry expectations level that might be associated with such a drastic disillusionment are not apparent.   Similarly the non-sandwich graduates from MANCON whose experience of work was highly congruent with what they expected ($t=2.06$, $p < .05$) compared with their counterparts in other companies, had a mean level of expectations slightly over the average.

Control variables

Also shown in table 5.2 are the means for some of the control variables which relate to the work experience of subjects. Comparison across companies reveals some interesting variances.   Social integration with work colleagues is perceived as significantly absent at BR ($t=3.35$ $p < .001$).   In terms of progressing their graduates toward satisfactory work placements   BGAS   is   least   successful ($t=1.73$, $p < .10$) but is one of the better companies when it comes to providing individuals with performance feedback ($t=5.53$, $p < .001$), along with KELL ($t=7.19$, $p < .001$). In contrast MANCON and BP are significantly poor in this area.   The sample mean for evaluation of company induction and training is 3.4 on a scale of five, and most organizations are close to this average with the exception of KELL, whose graduates rate this significantly low (t=3.91, p <.001). Perhaps compensating, their graduates are comparatively well paid, together with those working for BP.

Dependent Variables

Dealing with the whole graduate intake of each company (table 5.2), graduates at BP emerge most favourably both in their satisfaction with the job (t=2.67, p<.001) and commitment to the company (t=2.74, p<.001). In contrast the KELL subsample are least satisfied with a mean score dramatically below the sample average (t=6.33, p < .001). Once again the sandwich/non-sandwich breakdown illuminates these findings a little further. Table 5.3 reveals for instance that BR non-sandwich employees are more satisfied than their own non-sandwich contemporaries; and it is the non-sandwich contingent of the BP intake that accounts for this company's high mean score for job satisfaction, whereas their sandwich graduates are responsible for the high organizational commitment score. Also disguised by the overall figures is the fact that GEC sandwich and MANCON non-sandwich graduates are relatively well-satisfied, though not significantly, and MANCON non-sandwich are significantly more committed to their employee than other non-sandwich graduates (t=2.91, p<.001).

ANALYSIS OF RESULTS BY COMPANY

Up to this point the variances between the seven organizations on certain key variables have been discussed in a fairly descriptive manner, the purpose being comparative rather than analytical. But what does this data have to say in relation to the research hypotheses? Are there any consistent patterns within and across companies which confirm the effects of expectations and job choice factors upon subsequent job satisfaction and organization commitment? It must be emphasised that tables 5.2 and 5.3 are simply a re-arrangement of the frequencies data in such a way as to facilitate the examination of means and variances of crucial individual variables among a number of sample sub-groups; such a statistical breakdown is designed to yield information concerning the comparison of means across sub-samples rather than the nature of relationships between variables within sub-samples. However, with this important qualification in mind, it is permissable to detect some interesting patterns of statistical significance which at least suggest the lines of enquiry to follow.

The effects of independent variables upon dependent variables

Referring again to tables 5.2 and 5.3 and taking each company in turn several tentative conclusions can be drawn about how the circumstances of job choice and the nature of expectations influence graduates' attitudes to work.   For instance, while the variance from the sample mean for BR graduates is not significant on job satisfaction or organizational commitment, non-sandwich graduates do register significantly high job satisfaction;   there is no significant variance on other variables, except for low social integration, which suggests that the determinants of these favourable job attitudes are to be found in variables not measured here.   In GEC it is the sandwich graduates whose satisfaction is high - though not at a significant level. Possibly associated with this is the low discrepancy score for this subgroup, since the matching hypothesis predicts a relationship between met expectations and job satisfaction.   For these same sandwich graduates the influence of others in the job choice is significantly high (t=1.85, p < .10);   however according to the retrospective justification theory, such external constraint would reduce, not enhance, job satisfaction.

Moving on to BGAS, the mean profile for their graduates does not differ significantly from the overall sample mean for any variable except performance feedback: this control variable is significantly high but with no apparent effect on either of the dependent variables.   The most notable pattern of relationships is at BP.   Here graduate entrants express a great deal more job satisfaction (t=2.67, p < .001) and organizational commitment (t=2.74, p < .001) than any others. Alongside this positive picture BP sandwich graduates also had a greater number of job alternatives (t=2.52, p < .10) and their mean rank preference was also dramatically higher (t=3.80, p < .001). The association of both these job choice factors with relatively high job satisfaction and significantly high organizational commitment (t=1.85, p <.10) lends credence to the retrospective justification model, since greater freedom of choice is postulated to result in favourable job attitudes and behaviours.   However, the matching model is also in evidence, since for BP non-sandwich graduates significantly low discrepancy of expectations is accompanied by high job satisfaction.   Research has consistently found graduates' pre-entry expectations to be high and unrealistic and as a result of the mismatch with organizational reality, job satisfaction and organizational commitment low.   It is surprising to find then that the comparatively high mean scores for level of pre-entry level of expectations for graduates at BP (and for sandwich graduates

this was very significant) is not associated with high
incongruence and subsequent job dissatisfaction, in fact the
opposite holds true for this organization. This suggests that
either the 'level of expectations' variables used here is
measuring something other than accuracy or realism of
expectations prior to work entry, or that the traditional
matching expectations theory is to be questioned; a third
possibility is that the unusually high expectations of both
sandwich and non-sandwich BP graduates were untypically
fulfilled as indicated by the low discrepancy scores and
consequently the dependent variables rated highly.

KELL contrasts strikingly with BP: job satisfaction was
significantly lower for graduates in this organization than
any other of the companies (t=6.33, p <.001): for non-sandwich
entrants this can be attributed to either of the hypotheses :
since on the one hand rank preference was low, which would be
construed by retrospective justification theory as an external
constraint inhibiting the consequential expression of job
satisfaction, and on the other hand, the mean for weighted
discrepancy is very high (t=3.85, p< .001) and this would also
lead to low satisfaction according to the matching model. The
explanation of KELL sandwich graduates' is less
straightforward since two job choice factors had significant
variance from the overall mean : while the number of job
alternatives was very low at the time of choice, the rank
preference was significantly high. It seems that these
sandwich graduates were in one sense constrained by lack of
choice, yet still exercised autonomy since the one alternative
open to them was their first preference. However the base
number in this particular subsample is very small, so any
interpretation should be made with caution.

Graduates from MAN evinced only minimal differences from the
sample mean on all variables. Organizational commitment for
non-sandwich graduates at MANCON was significantly higher
(t=2.91, p<.001) than at other companies; job satisfaction
was high too, but not significantly so. To what might this be
attributed? A scan of the other mean scores for this subgroup
shows that these non-sandwich graduates also experienced
significantly low discrepancy between what they expected and
what they found in the companies they joined (t=2.06, p < .01)
– a finding which would support the matching hypothesis. This
subgroup also registered significantly low autonomy when
choosing their job (t=1.80, p< .05), possibly associated with
market pressure also indicated. In this case, then, the
retrospective justification hypothesis is not borne out
because high external constraint over the employment decision
should lead to less, not more, positive commitment to the

chosen company.

Drawing together these findings a number of tentative comments can be made concerning the research hypotheses under investigation:

(1) All significant variances on the mean scores for the job choice and weighted discrepancy variables are accompanied by a significant impact on one or both of the dependent variables.

This suggests that these factors do indeed have an important, though not necessarily exclusive, influence upon the satisfaction and commitment of graduate entrants.

(2) The level of expectations variable, on the other hand, does not appear to have any consistent impact on the dependent variables : it is either significantly low but with no manifest effect (GEC, non-sandwich); significantly high but associated with job satisfaction and commitment (BP sandwich and non-sandwich); or significantly low with concomitantly low satisfaction (KELL sandwich). In other words where there is an apparent effect, it runs counter to the prediction of the matching hypothesis.

(3) In every instance where significant differences are recorded on the dependent variables there are also significant variances on one or more of the independent variables. It is likely therefore that, between them, the job choice and expectation variables account for most of the variation in expressed job satisfaction and commitment across all the companies in the sample, sandwich and non-sandwich.

(4) If each significant variance is noted with reference to the primary research hypotheses (which are based on two theoretical premises) then the following preliminary assessment can be made: both hypotheses are supported by the BP sandwich and non-sandwich samples, where high satisfaction/commitment can be attributed to either high freedom of choice and/or low weighted discrepancy. In addition there is evidence for the matching hypotheses in MANCON non-sandwich graduates, who express high commitment and low discrepancy, and with KELL graduates (3) where very low job satisfaction is accompanied by a dramatically high mismatch. The retrospective justification hypothesis is not supported by the MANCON sample where high market pressure has no apparent negative impact on the dependent variables for non-sandwich graduates, and their sandwich colleagues express high organizational commitment despite high external influence when choosing the job.

WHERE DO DISCREPANCIES OCCUR?

A noticeable feature of table 5.2 is the expectations score : while there is no remarkable deviation from the overall mean of 72.3 for level of expectations for any of the seven companies, the mean scores for weighted discrepancy fluctuate extensively. In all cases there is a negative contrast between pre-entry expectations and actual experience in the organization; however for the graduates of some companies this discrepancy is particularly sharp. This raises two related questions : what aspects of the new job are responsible for bringing about such changes in perception, and what factors can explain the variability of their 'reality shock' from one company to another? Obviously, any findings that can shed light on these questions will be of great interest to all concerned with the effective integration of graduate employees. It was for this reason that the expectations/experience inventory was designed, to capture an appraisal of most, if not all, features of the new job and organizational climates, such that a mismatch between what a newcomer anticipated in his work and what he actually encountered could be identified and measured over 20 separate items. Having collected this information it is now feasible to compare in detail the differential experience of new entrants, first according to their employer company and second, according to the nature of their undergraduate training, either sandwich or full-time.

By company

Job and work expectations divided into three categories, describing the job itself, work-related aspects and the wider organizational climate. The job itself covers those expectations pertaining to the intrinsic nature of the work peformed : whether individual training is given on the job, how varied and interesting the work is, the extent to which the individual can use his abilities, the amount of responsibility, the degree of intellectual challenges, the pressure entailed in the job and finally whether it involves being in charge of other people. Work-related aspects concern wider, more extrinsic features of the job; included here are career prospects within the company, ease of movement between departments/locations, salary level, flexibility of working hours, working conditions, the opportunity to travel, the degree to which the further professional training is encouraged and finally, the friendliness of the department. Organizational aspects extend even wider to expectations concerning the macro climate of the company : the perceived fairness of company policies, management concern for people, security of tenure and the standard of recreational facilities provided by the employer.

Table 5.4 summarises the discrepancies between expectations and experience over these 20 job/organizational features across all companies. The prevailing impression is one of unmet expectations with only isolated instances where experience of job feature exceeds anticipation. Significantly, some aspects of the new work environment most discrepant with expectations were the intrinsic features, use of abilities and intellectual challenge for instance, that subjects elsewhere ranked as the two most important job features to them. Experience of individual training and the amount of responsibility in the job were also scored unfavourably in comparison with expectations across all companies. However some of the widest discrepancies occurred in relation to the wider organizational climate, although these tended to be linked to one or two companies rather than being consistent across the whole sample. Generally speaking work related features conformed most closely to pre-entry expectations : this is reasonable, and compatible with previous literature (Wanous 1976; Dunette, Arvey and Banas 1973) which has found such things as salary, work conditions and opportunities for professional training meeting expectations because they are more easily identified before employment commences.

By sandwich/non-sandwich

Over most aspects of job and organizational climates non-sandwich graduates have a higher level of expectations than their sandwich counterparts, with an overall mean of 3.9 on a five point scale compared wth 3.6, respectively. Prior experience of work, in terms of industrial sandwich placements, appears to have the effect of lowering expectations perhaps bringing them to a more realistic level; and this is particularly the case for intrinsic features of the work, variety, intellectual challenge, opportunity to use abilities and amount of pressure, as well as degree of movement within the workplace. In contrast, sandwich graduates are more optimistic at time one concerning opportunities for travel, amount of security and quality of recreational facilities provided by their respective companies. This is apparently based on first hand knowledge of the organizations concerned, yet in the first two of these three areas expectations proved, unaccountably, to be discrepant with reality to a high degree.

Turning to the mean scores for experience once with the

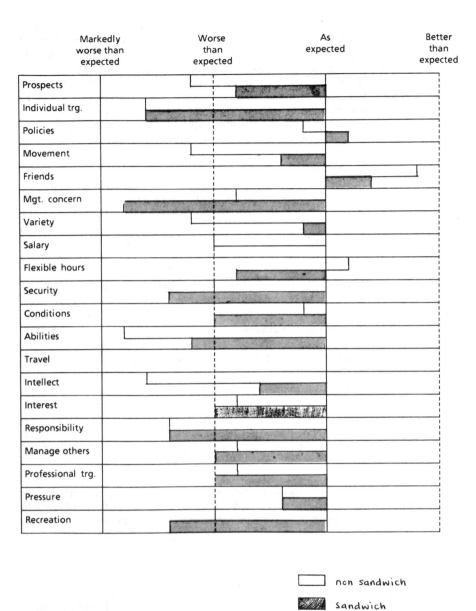

	Markedly worse than expected	Worse than expected	As expected	Better than expected

- Prospects
- Individual trg.
- Policies
- Movement
- Friends
- Mgt. concern
- Variety
- Salary
- Flexible hours
- Security
- Conditions
- Abilities
- Travel
- Intellect
- Interest
- Responsibility
- Manage others
- Professional trg.
- Pressure
- Recreation

☐ non sandwich

▨ sandwich

Figure 5.4 The discrepancies between expectations and experience by sandwich training, over 20 job features

company, the general trend is for a marked discrepancy with corresponding scores for each item. Although this is greater for non-sandwich graduates, where the average discrepancy over the 20 items is 0.6, the lack of congruence with expectations also holds true for sandwich graduates (0.5 over 20 items). What this indicates is a narrowing of the gap between sandwich and non-sandwich graduates over this transition period : while, before entry non-sandwich expectations are appreciably higher and, it could be argued, less realistic, than their sandwich contemporaries, yet after about six months work experience, their descriptive rating of the same 20 items is still slightly higher than those with sandwich training (3.3 as against 3.2 on a five point scale) (4). Two exceptions to this are travel and intellectual challenge which sandwich students rate higher. For all graduates the major discrepancies take place in the areas of individual training, use of abilities, amount of responsibility and interesting work; non-sandwich graduates also indicate discrepancies concerning movement and intellectual challenge; while for sandwich graduates recreation facilities and management concern fall below expectations.

Again, the key points could be summarised as follows:

(1) There is a negative discrepancy for both sandwich and non-sandwich graduates over the whole range of job/organizational features. In only isolated instances does experience on the job prove to be better than expected. This inflated pre-entry picture is in accord with the literature (Ward and Athos 1972; Bray, Campbell and Grant 1973).

(2) The degree of this discrepancy is definitely greater for non-sandwich graduates. This suggests that a degree of prior work experience in the form of industrial placements reduces discrepancy, and this is a potentially important factor in determining future job satisfaction and organizational commitment.

(3) Significantly, the greatest discrepancy tends to occur in those aspects of the job most important to the individual such as use of abilities and intellectual challenge. Again this corroborates the findings of similar graduate studies (Dunette et al 1973; Wanous 1976).

NOTES

(1) It is to be expected that sandwich students would have a narrower range of job options since, for the most part, there

would have been no active consideration of other employers other than the one where industrial placements were spent. This is reflected in the low mean scores of sandwich students for this variable across all companies.

(2) With the exception of external influence on job choice for GEC sandwich graduates, and high market pressure on MANCON graduates.

(3) The KELL sample is taken as a whole because the total sample is just ten.

(4)Their overall mean score for experience of the 20 items is slightly greater than that of sandwich graduates, but their perceived discrepancy is also greater, which is the important one for the matching hypothesis.

6 Realism

The preceding discussion has helped to establish that not only do graduates typically find their expectation of work unmatched once they are employed, but also which aspects are most prone to discrepancy and the degree to which this is influenced by type of company and type of undergraduate training.   Tentative comments have also been made concerning the associations between both expectations and job choice variables and differences in job response between different company subsamples.   These suggested relationships can now be taken up and scrutinized more carefully in order to test the seven hypotheses arising from the research model.   These hypothesised effects upon the dependent variables will be analysed in turn,   looking first at the two strands of the expectations variables – congruency and realism – and then at the impact of autonomy of job choice.

THE CONGRUENCY OF EXPECTATIONS VARIABLES

Each of the variables measuring congruency of expectations was deduced from the expectations index of 20 job and organizational items on questionnaire one and the corresponding experience index on questionnaire two, and as shown in table 6.1 the three variables associate very highly with each other.   For instance, the degree of exact matches between expectations and experience, is correlated significantly with the number of weighted mismatches, (T=-.35, p<.001);   since these are two sides of the same coin it would

TABLE 6.1 - Intercorrelation between independent variables (Kendall's T)

VARIABLE		1	2	3	4	5	6	7	8	9	10	11
JOB CHOICE												
Job alternatives	1											
market pressure*	2	-.099*										
external constraints	3	.073	-.059									
rank preference*	4	.003	.288°°	.017°								
Irrevocability	5	-.157°°	.241°°°	.004	.017							
EXPECTATIONS CONGRUENCE												
match	6	-.105*	-.018	-.108*	-.134	.057						
mismatch*	7	-.011	.186°°	.124°	.097	-.003	-.351°°°					
discrepancy*	8	.066	.117*	-.038	.051	.051	-.274°°°	.242°°°				
EXPECTATIONS: REALISM												
pre-entry level	9	.073	-.034	.113*	-.104	-.144°	.081	.173°°	.723°°°			
industrial work	10	-.028	-.001	-.020	-.049	-.082	.004	.000	.004	-.049		
prior work with company.	11	-.179°°°	-.120°	-.190°	.142°	-.058	.205°°°	-.126*	-.089	-.092*	.375°°°	

*P < .05

°P < .01

°°P < .005

°°°P < .001

* Reverse scored

be unusual if there were not a high negative correlation between them: the higher degree of match the lower the incidence of mismatches and vice versa. Also, as would be anticipated, the measure of weighted disrepancy, is highly correlated with mismatched expectations where the direction of the relationship is positive (T=.24, p< .001) and with match where it is negative (T=-.27, p <.001) (1).

The effects of congruent expectations upon dependent variables

Matched expectations have a positive effect on each of the job satisfaction measures (table 6.2). Most striking is the crosstabulation between matched expectations and overall satisfaction which shows that graduates who secured a greater number of exact matches between what they anticipated and actually encountered in their work were no less than six times more likely to register satisfaction with the job, representing a highly significant correlation (T=.255, p < .001). The contingency table reveals a similar positive pattern of relationships with the other aspects of satisfaction.

The influence upon job satisfaction of mismatched expectations for job items important to the subject is even greater. Crosstabulations show a strong negative association between the number of such mismatches and degree of satisfaction for all four of the measures, the correlation being significant at the p <.001 level in each case. The enhancing effect of low incidence of mismatches upon global satisfaction is especially pronounced; more than five times as many graduates express high job satisfaction when the number of mismatches they have experienced is low than when the number is high. For the other job satisfaction dimensions it is the <u>high</u> number of mismatches that is the critical feature: here, the percentage expressing low job satisfaction is twice as great or more. A similar pattern, though slightly muted, holds for the effects of this variable upon organizational commitment. In that the values for pre-entry expectations and post-entry experience are weighted according to their relative importance to the subject at the respective times, the weighted discrepancy measure is undoubtedly the most precise of those assesssing congruency since it has a subjective element built into it. Hence it is all the more significant that the association between this measure and job satisfaction is also the most dramatic and sensitive, (p <.001) in each case. Weighted discrepancy also correlates highly with the five dimensions of organizational commitment, but the significance levels are lower.

	JOB SATISFACTION				ORGANIZATION COMMITMENT				
	overall satisf'n	prefer to move*	job satisf'n	weighted satisf'n	desire to stay	intended tenure*	general comm't	comm't to stay	values comm't
EXPECTATIONS: CONGRUENCE									
match	.255°°°	-.137°	.218°°°	.188°°°	.182°°°	-.149°°	.132°	.189°°°	.098*
mismatch*	-.320°°°	.257°°°	-.334°°°	-.3339°°°	-.221°°°	.151°°	-.122*	-.122*	-.119°
discrepancy*	-.391°°°	.293°°°	-.406°°°	-.365°°°	-.185°°°	.154°°	-.204°°°	-.164°°	-.178°°
EXPECTATIONS: REALISM									
pre-entry level	.151°°	-.082	.156°°	.125*	.185°°°	-.244°°°	.258°°°	.228°°°	.268°°°
industrial work	-.141°	.151°°	-.057	-.056	-.187°°°	.190°°°	-.158°°	-.142°	-.154°°
prior work with company	-.031	.147°	-.075	-.063	-.074	.092	-.128°	-.062	-.150°°

*P < .05

°P < .01

°°P < .005

°°°P < .001

* reverse scored

Undoubtedly the congruency of a graduate's expectations with what he actually encounters in his new workplace has an important bearing on his expressed satisfaction and commitment to that job. This is apparent from the above findings, which could be summarised in the following way:

(1) The three measures of congruency correlate significantly with all dimensions of the dependent variables.

(2) Crosstabulations reveal that these relationships are in the direction hypothesised: matched expectations are positively associated with, and mismatch and weighted discrepancy are negatively associated with, the dependent variables.

(3) As the measures become more sensitive, so the correlations become more intense; mismatch, which takes account of self-reported importance rankings is stronger than match, and weighted discrepancy which embraces these rankings in both the before and after measures demonstrates the strongest relationships of all.

(4) The impact of congruent expectations is particularly pronounced upon job satisfaction.

The last observation raises a possible question: can this very significant pattern of correlations be explained by the fact that the variables, though treated as independent and dependent, are in fact measuring the same thing? In other words, is not matched expectations essentially similar to job satisfaction? Inevitably there is a degree of overlap between these two variables, but they can be regarded as conceptually distinct in this study for two reasons. First, the wording of the expectations inventory at time one and the corresponding experience inventory at time two explicitly call for a descriptive response, asking the subject to rate the accuracy of a number of statements in a non-evaluative manner. As will be discovered in the discussion of the level of expectations variable, respondents are influenced by what they hope for in their future job as much as what they really know about the organization, leading to an overly positive picture; but there is no reason to suspect that the ratings on the experience inventory at time two are anything other than a descripton of job facets as they are. That assessment of organizational climate can be utilised as an independent variable to observe its differential impact on job satisfaction, has been argued by Schneider (1975b). Second, the three expectations measures in question concern the discrepancy or congruence of expectations over a period of about six months with organizational reality. Such a research design avoids the pitfalls of other 'one-shot' methodologies that have relied upon a single recollected measure of pre-entry expectations (for instance, 'Is your experience of item A better or worse than you expected?") and then correlated this with job satisfaction (Dunette, Arvey and Banas 1973).

Given, then, that the instrument is valid, why is it that matched expectations bring about such a positive response to the job, and to a lesser extent, commitment to the organization? Certainly this finding is consistent with the postulations of the 'unmet expectations' literature (Ross and Zander 1957; Katzell 1968; Dunette et al 1973), which has attributed dissatisfaction and turnover to disconfirmed expectations, similar to the 'broken promise' effect. Although these studies failed to account for over met expectations which may compensate or at least attenuate the negative response (2), the explanation has intuitive appeal: graduate newcomers register their disenchantment because what they hoped for in the job has not materialised. Perhaps their early months of employment have not fulfilled the inflated prospects inculcated by the recruitment and induction process, and whether or not they were responsible for instilling this unhealthy optimism, the graduate feels cheated by his employer.

Further understanding of this process can be gleaned by noting the way the congruency variables interrelate with the other independent and control variables. It is found for instance in table 6.1 that high match is associated with a low number of job alternatives (T=-.10, p < .05). This could be interpreted in two ways: the constrained choice could either lead the graduate to lower his expectations (realising that he is unlikely to have his job ideals met to the degree he would wish) to a more realistic level, which in turn are more likely to be matched. This argument borrows from the rationale of the unrealistic expectations hypotheses which will be considered next. Alternatively the connection between low job choice and poor job satisfaction and commitment is also consistent with the retrospective justification hypothesis, whereby the negative job response is due not so much to poor match as the low degree of autonomy exercised in securing the job in the first place, which leads to indifferent personal commitment to the chosen options. Indeed, there is no reason why both mechanisms should not be in operation, since they do not mutually exclude each other.

Reference to the control variables which correlate with match (table 6.3) suggests that the former of these two explanations

TABLE 6.3 -Correlation between work related controls and expectations (Kendall's T)

	prior contact with co	plans to stay	previous work experience	quantity of job info	quality of job info
EXPECTATIONS					
Discrepancy*	.069	.050	.073	.026	.006
Pre-entry Level	.71°°	.342°°°	.046	.152°°	.178°°
Match	.084	.035	-.046	.266°°°	.133°
Mismatch*	.011	.006	.165°	-.054	-.045

*P<.05 °P<.01 °°P<.005 °°°P<.001

* reverse scored

is better supported here. Matched expectations correlate highly with both quantity ($T=.266$, $p <.001$) and quality of information prior to entry ($T=.133$, $p <.01$); further a high correlation is found between matched expectations and another expectations variable, which taps the amount of time previously spent in related work ($T=.203$, $p< .001$) as show in table 6.1. The combined force of these three relationships suggest that the element of realism contained in the matched expectations variable is indeed high based on both relevant work experience and the quality/quantity of prior knowledge about the company. A similar pattern of associations exists with mismatch, except in the reverse direction to match, as would be predicted: low mismatch correlates significantly with low level of expectations ($T=.173$, $p < .005$) and greater time spent in related work ($T=-.126$, $p < .05$): in other words the mismatch measure, like its mirror variable, match, appears to authentically reflect realistic expectations since a high level of expectations and/or minimal previous work experience would both contribute to a greater mismatch.

Finally, the third dimension of match, weighted discrepancy, confirms this picture. Table 6.1 shows a high positive correlation between discrepancy of expectations ($T=.723$, $p < .001$). Formulated negatively this indicates that low disrepancy of expectations is associated with low level of expectations; indeed since the variable 'level' chronologically precedes the one tapping 'disrepancy', it could be suggested that the level of expectations actually influences the degree of subsequent congruency.

Summary and conclusions

It has been clearly and comprehensively demonstrated that the congruence of pre-work expectations, (measured by match, mismatch and weighted disrepancy) with post-entry experience of the same job features positively relates to graduates' expression of job satisfaction and organizational commitment. This finding confirms our first hypothesis. In seeking an explanation for this set of relationships by reference to other variables there is good reason for believing that the matching occurs because the initial expectations are lower and more realistic than they are for those graduates who do not experience matched expectations; the consequence is more positive feelings towards their job and greater loyalty to their company. The gap between what an individual hopes for and what he encounters in the way of pleasant or disenchanting surprises in the job appears to provide a valuable indicator of his affective response to the organization six months or so after entry. While this validates the unmet expectations hypothesis, found in the literature, it has incidentally been established that high match and low discrepancy reflect the respective degrees of realism present in a graduate's expectations as he approaches employment. Whether the existence of realistic expectations has a direct bearing on the dependent variables is the subject of the next section.

REALISM OF EXPECTATIONS VARIABLES

Originally, realism of expectations was to be assessed by the level of expectations variable alone, comprising a summation of 20 specific pre-entry expectations. However the variables measuring the amount of previous, related work experience, and the length of time worked with the company prior to full-time employment, were found to be very appropriate measures of the accuracy of pre-entry expectations and were subsequently utilised alongside the level of expectations variable. Table 6.1 shows a small correlation between level and prior work with company (T=-.092, p <.05), but no relationship between level and industrial work. In constrast the correlation coefficient summarising the relationship between industrial work and prior work with company is very high (T=.375, p <.001). This is not at all surprising since the high industrial work variable represents all those subjects with six months or more relevant industrial experience; analysis of the frequency tables reveals that this, by definition, includes all sandwich students in the sample (54) whose placements would always exceed this period of time, together with a further six non-sandwich students who had extensive experience in related work. Breaking the 'work with company' variable down in a similar way shows that from the 135 in the total sample, 106 had no prior experience of work with their employer, and 29 had three months or more such exposure. Of these 25 were sponsored by their respective companies, the remaining four via ad hoc industrial placements. Figure 6.1 outlines the derivation of these variables.

Broadly speaking, we could say first, that those with 'high' industrial work scores are equivalent to all sandwich students plus six non sandwich graduates whose work experience nevertheless puts them on a par with sandwich experience; second, those high on the 'work with company' variable constitute the sponsored students in the sample, together with four others whose industrial exposure is so relevant as to merit assigning them this status (3). It should now be evident that the two variables provide valuable indicators of realism: industrial work on a general work experience level and work with company in a way that is more organization

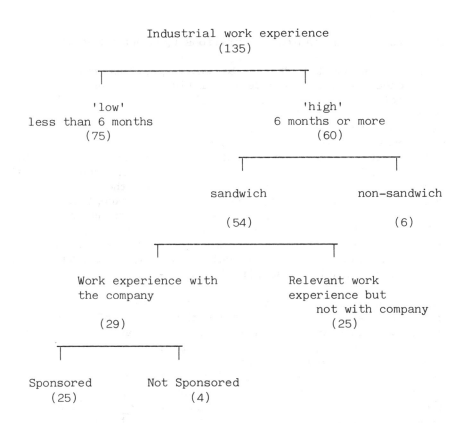

Industrial work experience
(135)

'low'
less than 6 months
(75)

'high'
6 months or more
(60)

sandwich
(54)

non-sandwich
(6)

Work experience with
the company
(29)

Relevant work
experience but
not with company
(25)

Sponsored
(25)

Not Sponsored
(4)

Figure 6.1 The type and proportions of previous work
experienced by the sample

specific.

The effect of realism of expectations upon dependent variables

Table 6.2 shows the degree to which previous related work experience and/or placements influences subsequent job satisfaction. For two of the satisfaction measures there is evidence of a negative relationship, such that those with little work experience are proportionately more likely to also be those expressing high overall job satisfaction ($T=-.141$, $p <.01$) and low preference to move jobs ($T=.151$, $p < .005$).The impact of this variable upon organizational commitment is even stronger. Again the pattern of relationships is negative, and in each case except commitment to stay it is significant. The noticeable trend is to find those with little prior work experience expressing greater organizational commitment on the intended tenure, general commitment and values commitment variables, the proportions being almost double those with low commitment.

However for desire to stay and commitment to stay, high prior work experience appears to have the effect of drastically reducing this commitment such that in the case of the former graduates they are nearly four times less likely to be committed to their employers. All five dimensions of organizational commitment correlate negatively with high work experience at .01 level of significance or greater. These findings demonstrate clearly that the less related work experience graduates have prior to organizational entry the more likely they are to be satisfied with their jobs overall, the less inclined they will be to move elsewhere and the more bound they will be to their employer in terms of both values and tenure commitment. If exposure to prior, relevant industrial experience provides a genuine gauge of the accuracy or realism of an individual's pre-entry expectations - and there is no reason to doubt that it does - then the effects of unrealistic expectations do not have the negative influence predicted by the literature and hypothesised in this research: for it is those without the benefit of a realistic preview who express the greater contentment!

As anticipated the pattern of association with the dependent variables exhibited by those who have actually worked with the company as students broadly shadows that of those with previous industrial experience. For instance, the negative association with job satisfaction is not so great, though it is most noticeable in the contingency table with preference to move, where the proportion of those wanting to move is twice that of those happy to stay when time was spent with the company prior to graduation. Significant correlations are found between previous work and values commitment (T=-.150, p < .005) and also with general commitment (T=-.128, p < .01). So although slightly less emphatic than with its related variable of industrial experience, prior work with the organization appears not to enhance subsequent commitment and job satisfaction, indeed it is those without such exposure who evince the more positive response.

Turning to the third and original measure of realism, pre-entry level of expectations, the pattern of relationships becomes even more fascinating.

There are positive relationships between expectations level and overall satisfaction (T= .151, p< .005), job satisfaction (T=.156, p <.005) and weighted satisfaction (T= .125, p < .05). The impact of a high level of expectations upon organizational commitment reinforces this pattern. Four out of the five organizational commitment dimensions are significantly associated with the initial level of expectations, and the positive direction of these relationships is distinct in each of the contingency tables. When their expectation level is high graduates are twice as likely to be committed to their employer and when this pre-entry level is low the negative effect is most pronounced for the desire and commitment to stay variables where the proportion of graduates not committed to staying with the company is more than three times greater than those who are. The Kendall test of significance confirms this with highly significant correlations across all five dimensions (p< .001). So, far from creating dissatisfaction and low organizational commitment, the prevailing effect of a high level of pre-entry expectations is a positive association with the dependent variables. As noted by Louis (1980), previous researchers testing the effects of realistic expectations have usually operationalised this as 'merely the inverse of expectation level, lower expectations are considered more realistic than are high expectations' (p.228). So the findings here run counter to this strand of literature which would argue that a high level of pre-entry expectations indicates lack of realism, unrealistic expectations are less likely to be fulfilled on the job, resulting in low satisfaction and voluntary turnover follow.

In assessing the effects of this set of 'realism' variables on job satisfaction and organizational commitment we find that each has not only failed to confirm our second hypothesis, but the evidence is fairly convincing that these variables actually contradict the hypothesised relationships. Again, examination of the influence of other variables will help to explain why this is the case. Taking level of expectations first, how is it that a high level of pre-entry expectations is correlated with high job satisfaction and organizational commitment, when the opposite was predicted? Whilst it was intended that level would provide a comprehensive measure of pre-entry realism, based as it is on the graduate's perceived accuracy of 20 statements concerning his prospective employer, it is inevitable that what an individual hopes for his job will colour the way he responds to this index. This is even more likely if company information is sparse; although there is a category for 'don't know at this stage' it is natural at this pre-entry stage (when post-choice dissonance is intense) for respondents to give their chosen employer the benefit of the doubt and record favourable impressions, based on optimism rather than well founded knowledge. This interpretation is confirmed by relationships between level and control variables relating to pre-entry attitudes and information (table 6.3). For instance level of expectations is highly correlated with the amount ($T= .152$, $p < .005$) and quality ($T= .178$, $p < .001$) of job information available before job entry. Superficially, these could be taken as indications of realism, but these assessments of company information are as perceived by the subject and open to the same optimistic inference as the level measure itself. This perception of high knowledge, which is not necessarily accurate or complete, is further bolstered by the high correlation with the variable which measures the degree of prior contact with the company through interviews and visits ($T= .171$, $p < .005$). Finally, it can be seen that level is also positively correlated with the intention of staying with the company long-term, ($T= .342$, $p < .001$).

Possibly then, this cluster of variables tells us more about the tone of the individual's aspirations concerning his future employment than the realism of his expectations. That the graduate's expectations are in fact less than accurate, despite these positive evaluations of job information and intended tenure, is borne out even more clearly by the intercorrelation with other expectations variables (table 6.1): level of expectations is positively correlated with higher mismatch and higher weighted discrepancy at .005 and .001 significance levels, respectively, suggesting that the poor match of expectations with experience is due (in part) to the inflated level prior to entry. Further evidence comes from the negative correlation between level and prior work with the company ($T=-.092$, $p < .05$), and between level and the sandwich ($X^2 =4.84$, $p <.05$) and sponsorship variables ($X^2 =4.13$, $p < .05$) as shown in table 6.4. Having worked with the company, being a sandwich student and/or being sponsored can all be regarded as yardsticks of realism, since these variables imply first-hand exposure to the organization concerned or at least related work experience. The fact that level relates negatively with each one underlines the conclusion that 'level of expectations' reflects not so much the graduate's accuracy of expectations as the degree of optimism he possesses as he enters employment.

If this is the case, why does such optimism - or lack of realism - appear to result in an enhanced, rather than a deflated evaluation of the job several months after entry? One explanation lies in the relationship between level and the job choice variables which were also assessed at time one. Table 6.1 shows that high level is correlated with high autonomy in the form of freedom from external pressure, (T=.113, p <.05). Though unexpected this relationship is very significant because, in line with the retrospective justification reasoning, it introduces a crucial factor into the picture: that of commitment, which follows from making a highly autonomous choice. Such a finding is consistent with the previous observation of the very high correlation between level and long-term plans to stay, which also suggests high commitment even at a pre-entry stage (4). Indeed it would not be unreasonable to regard tenure intention as an aspect of perceived autonomy, since making a statement concerning long-term commitment to the organization at time one could be interpreted, along with the other job choice variables, as a binding act which would propel the graduate toward committed behaviours.

The one piece of evidence contrary to the thrust of this argument is the correlation between level and irrevocability (T=.144, p < .01), whereby high level of expectations is associated with high revocability at time one. However this sense of being able to change jobs easily has disappeared by time two (T=.024 n/s) which is when the dependent variables are measured, and since it is the present existence of other job opportunities that is the crucial aspect of irrevocability (Pfeffer and Lawler 1980), this contradiction may be less critical. Furthermore revocability as measured at time one fails to relate to any of the dependent variables. Leaving this one exception aside then, our understanding of the level of expectations variable is extended in that it can be closely and positively related to autonomy, such that high level of expectations is associated with high freedom of choice and high tenure intention. Such attitudes would naturally combine together in producing and indicating commitment, which would be reflected in positive responses to work and the company.

Another explanation, is that a high level of pre-entry

expectations simply signifies a positive and confident mentality, and despite major discrepancies between what was hoped for and what is encountered at the workplace, the individual remains optimistic, perhaps having adjusted his ideals in the face of unpleasant reality, and consequently expresses satisfaction and commitment in keeping with his outlook. To verify this would require the assistance of some kind of personality assessment, yet the argument is not unrelated, nor inconsistent, with the earlier assertion that perceived autonomy enhances commitment to the course of action, which in turn has a positive effect on job attitudes; although, how long these attitudes prevail despite unmatched expectations is not yet clear.

It was found that the effect of prior work experience and previous exposure to the company on the dependent variables was also in a direction not anticipated. To what can this be attributed? It has already been demonstrated that those high on the 'with company' variable are correlated with those who also experience a higher degree of matched expectations (T=.205, p < .001) and low mismatch (T=-.126, p <.05). This is no surprise: those with relevant work experience would be likely to know far more about the job they are entering and find more of their expectations being fulfilled. What is initially baffling is to find this realism not being translated into subsequent satisfaction and commitment. Once again, reference to the circumstances of job choice can help to provide a more complete picture. The negative correlation shown in table 6.1 between number of suitable job alternatives and experience with company is very high (T=-.179, p < .001); similarly there is a significant negative correlation between experience with company and the amount of external influence upon job choice (T=-.190, p < .05). By contrast the correlations with market pressure and rank preference are positively significant. The reasons behind these relationships are self-evident if it is remembered that those with much previous company experience represent, primarily, those with sandwich and/or sponsorship experience with the company concerned. Such graduates would, in most cases, have chosen their employer organization prior to university and therefore it would be natural to rank it high according to original personal preference, and by the same token, market pressures would be minimised. While these two factors would enhance autonomy (certainly at the time), the positive effects are likely to be offset by the other two job choice variables: the fact that it was chosen at such an early stage also increases the likelihood of external influence, especially parental, in the decision - which explains the high correlation with external constraints; and the fact that there

TABLE 6.4 - Association between biographical/education controls and expectations (X²)

	father's occup'n	secondary education	degree type	degree class	prior contact with co	sandwich training	sponsorship	general work experience
DISCREPANCY	0.33	1.91	2.45	0.66	1.47	.36	1.88	1.29
pre-entry level	0.63	8.63	3.82	.01	4.50•	4.84•	4.13•	0.50
industrial work	-	-	-	-	1.64	101.53°°°	35.64°°°	8.98°°
prior work with co.	-	-	-	-	1.49	25.91°°°	50.17°°°	7.73°°

•P<.01 °P<.02 °°P<.005 °°°P<.001

were few if any other job options present explains why the negative correlation with the job alternatives variable is so significant.

Furthermore it is reasonable to suggest that the effects of the latter two variables not only compensate but actually outweigh the former two since the positive salience of low market pressure and high rank preference have long since passed, indeed may have changed in the meantime. Why? Because the job market is now more competitive (making it difficult to change jobs even if this were possible) and experience of the chosen company has brought misgivings about the wisdom of the original ranking, so that rather than enhancing his sense of autonomy, these factors now conspire to constrain the sandwich graduate. As he assesses his employment prospects at graduation, he is actually aware of his lack of alternatives (due to a not-easily-revoked commitment to his sponsor) and the extent to which this was not his own, freely made decision in the first place. The presence of both these is reflected in the negative correlations with alternatives and external constraints. In short, despite original freeedom of choice in terms of rank and market pressure, the dominant feeling at the time of entry is one of high constraint.

This would explain the expression of low job satisfaction and organizational commitment. Despite the fact that pre-entry expectations are realistic and consequently matched, the job fulfilment and loyalty to the company that this would normally instil are overridden by the circumstances under which that job choice was made.

By way of summarising the effects of the realism of expectations measures, it has been discovered that:

(1)   Level of pre-entry expectations is more a reflection of optimistic anticipation than realistic expectations about the job and company.

(2)   The existence of a high level of prior expectations nevertheless leads to job satisfaction and organization commitment primarily because it is associated with greater autonomy of job choice and commitment to the course of action prior to entry.

(3)   Previous industrial experience and prior work with the
        company joined appear to be reliable indicators of pre-
        entry realism but graduates with a high degree of
        relevant, prior to work experience exhibit less job
        satisfaction and organization commitment because the
        very nature of their sandwich training limits their
        perceived freedom of choice when it comes to final entry
        into employment, and low autonomy deflates commitment to
        the company particularly, but also lowers job
        satisfaction.

These findings confound the predictions of hypothesis two.
However, monitoring the associated effects of relevant control
variables enables an explanation to be found which is largely
consistent with the total network of relationships and which
relies upon the retrospective justification theory. How the
research findings relate directly to this theory, and its
hypothesised implications concerning job entry, will now be
analysed.

NOTES

(1) T denotes the Kendall rank correlation coefficient.

(2) Overmet expectations were catered for in the design of the
expectation variables used here.

(3) Note that in constructing the variable this way a possible
pitfall has been avoided. If the sandwich/non-sandwich
split had been taken at face value in providing a measure
of pre-entry realism, the presence of non-sandwich
graduates who had nevertheless gained substantial, relevant
work experience may well have obscured any pattern of
relationships between realism and the dependent variables.

(4) The credence of this suggestion is substantiated by the
fact that long-term plans to stay correlate significantly
with three of the original job variables: job alternatives
($T=.130$, $p<.05$), market pressure ($T=.192$, $p<.001$) and rank
preference ($T=.126$, $p<.05$).

7 Autonomy

Although the five job choice variables tap different aspects of autonomy present at the time of this decision, it is not surprising to find in some cases that they are closely related (table 6.1). For instance, when market pressure was perceived as high, rank preference for the chosen job is significantly lower (T=.288, p < .001) and irrevocability is found to be higher (T=.241, p< .001) - both being symptoms of a highly competitive employment situation. Similarly number of job alternatives correlates negatively with market pressure (T=-.099, p <.05) and perceived irrevocability (T=-.157, p< .005): obviously when the range of choice is greater the constraints of the labour market are seen to be minimal, with the opportunity to change job easily if so desired. Finally, there is a significant correlation between external pressure and original rank, (T=.017, p<.01), whereby the rank of the job improves as the influence of other contributors to the decision diminishes. This pattern of intercorrelations is encouraging in that in each case the direction of the relationship confirms the validity of the measures being used, yet also supports the value of retaining them as separate variables as against O'Reilly and Caldwell (1981) who chose to combine their four dimensions of volitionality into a single index score.

Job Alternatives

Having a greater number of job alternatives to choose from has no significant impact on job satisfaction. Crosstabulations show that there is a far greater proportion of graduates registering overall satisfaction, but this is true of those with both high and low job choice. In the case of preference to move, the respondents are distributed almost equally in the four cells. The tables for job satisfaction and weighted satisfaction show a minor positive relationship with high number of job alternatives, but it is not significant. This positive association is much more apparent when 'job alternatives' is correlated with organizational commitment (table 7.1). Graduates having few alternatives at the time of job choice are more than three times less likely to want to remain with the company: whether this lack of commitment materialises into voluntary turnover is not known, but clearly the intention at this stage is to stay only short-term ($T=.140$, $p < .01$). With intended tenure, the noticeable contrast is on the positive side, such that those with greater perceived job choice, indicating further commitment, are nearly twice the proportion of those less certain about staying with their employer ($T=-.106$, $p < .05$) This association is less emphatic between number of alternatives and the other commitment variables, but once again the tables do reveal the same trend. Overall, then, there is fairly strong evidence that more job alternatives do enhance an individual's behavioural commitment to the chosen company, though the effects on attitudinal commitment are less distinct.

Market Pressure

According to hypothesis four, the greater perceived freedom from graduate labour market constraints, the more likely new entrants will express satisfaction and commitment to the chosen organization. Crosstabulations show that there is no such relationship for any of the dimensions with either job satisfaction and organizational commitment. Once again, the cell proportions reveal a very slight negative relationship in the predicted direction for most of the sub variables, but in no case is this nearing significance levels, either on the chi squared statistic or with Kendall rank correlation.

External Pressure

Likewise, the degree to which other contributors influenced the job choice decision has little impact on subsequent job satisfaction and organizational commitment. The left-hand column totals of the contingency tables reveal a relatively

Table 7.1 - Impact of job choice factors on job satisfaction and commitment (Kendall's T)

| | JOB SATISFACTION | | | | | ORGANIZATION COMMITMENT | | | | |
	overall satisf'n	prefer to move*	job satisf'n	weighted satisf'n	desire to stay	intended tenure*	general comm't	comm't to stay	values comm't
Job Alternatives	.036	.033	-.003	.023	.140°	-.106•	.020	.038	.019
Market Pressure*	.081	.060	-.081	-.057	-.065	.071	.028	-.028	-.025
External Constraints	.046	-.042	.053	.005	.138°	-.099•	.079	.060	.039
Rank Preference*	-.155°	-.181°°	-.133°	-.118•	.090	.044	.073	-.064	.096
Irrevocability	.009	-.150°°	-.042	-.026	.077	-.054	.004	.050	.008

•P < .05 °P < .01 °°P < .005 °°°P < .001

* Reversed Scored

106

low percentage of the sample who felt constrained in this way.

Rank Preference

When the chosen job is also one that was ranked highly in the subject's original preference, then he will express greater satisfaction with the job. This is evident from table 7.1 where rank preference is seen to correlate positively and significantly with each of the job satisfaction dimensions, the relationship being most significant with overall satisfaction (T=.-155, p < .01) and prefer to move (T=.181, p <.005). For instance, the proportion of those securing a high ranking job and indicating overall satisfaction is five times that of those expressing low satisfaction; conversely those whose employer was ranked low in terms of personal preference are almost twice as likely to prefer to move to another job than stay with the organization. Ranking plays a less important role in the determination of organizational commitment; however a slightly higher proportion of those with a highly ranked job also express high commitment for the desire to stay, intended tenure and values commitment variables.

Revocability

The fifth dimension of job choice concerns the perceived ease of changing jobs. Here the hypothesised relationship is that the more irrevocable the job choice the greater the satisfaction and commitment. The only evidence of this from table 7.1 is that between high irrevocability and low preference to move, (T=-.150, p < .01). It seems that perceived revocability at the time of choosing an employer has only a minor effect on a graduate's subsequent attachment to the company, albeit in the predicted direction.

Summary of job choice factors

When correlated with the various measures of organizational commitment, the two job choice variables which seem to have an impact are alternatives, and extent of external influence from others; and the impact is on the behavioural, as against the attitudinal, elements of organizational commitment. Having a higher number of jobs to choose from leads to a greater commitment to stay with the chosen company, together with the expressed intention to remain longer. Perceiving that the decision was also made autonomously (that is, free from the pressure of family and friends) is also associated with a similar degree of behavioural commitment to the organization.

Why is this? Each of the job choice variables constitute a form of external pressure; however, while market pressure and securing a high rank, which to some extent is tempered by the competitiveness of the labour market, are factors very much beyond the control of the individual, this is less true for the other two variables: number of alternatives and pressure from family and friends. In these latter cases, both represent potential constraints but it is up to the individual as to how much he allows them to influence his decision: he is the one who shortlists his final range of viable alternatives and he is the one who ultimately chooses to be coerced or not by the opinions of family and friends. It is thus consistent with the retrospective justification argument to find that those circumstances at the time of choice over which the subject has little control, influence subsequent behaviour less because the constraints are more extrinsic and do not require the degree of self justification as factors where there was a greater autonomy of choice. Such an interpretation would also explain why it is the behavioural dimension of organizational commitment that is affected. A graduate with a number of job offers and/or relative freedom from the constraints of outside contributors to the decision, states that he plans to stay longer with the chosen organization because not to do so would be inconsistent with his relatively autonomous decision; however there is no expressed attitudinal commitment to the organization since an identification with company values or stated loyalty to the chosen company is not required: it is sufficient that he registers his commitment in tenure plans alone. Indeed it could be argued that the individual is merely expressing commitment to his original freely chosen decision rather than commitment to the organization joined.

It is also interesting to note that the relationships of job alternatives and external constraints with other independent and control variables reinforce this retrospective justification explanation still further. For instance, having a high number of job offers is associated with a poor, rather than an improved, degree of match (T=-.105, p <.05) as shown in table 6.1. Despite this poor match, a high number of job offers still leads to job satisfaction, which is an effect opposite to that predicted by matched-expectations rational hypothesis. Perhaps the low match is offset by the influence of tenure intention which table 7.2 shows to correlate with number of alternatives (T=.130, p <.05), and time spent with the company or in related work which has a strong negative association with number of alternatives (T=.-179, p <.001). The combination of these two relationships suggests that the choice of company is 'fresh', that is, not based on prior

Table 7.2 - Correlation between work-related controls and job choice (Kendall's T)

	prior contact with co	plans to stay	previous work experience	quantity of job information	quality of job information
Job Alternatives	.050	.130°	.114•	-.125	.043
Market Pressure*	-.049	-.192°°°	.092•	-.094•	-.066
External Constraints	.045	.089	.107•	.037	.077
Rank Preference*	-.031	-.126•	.185°°	-.066	-.079
Irrevocability	-.033	-.012	-.039	-.038	-.189°°°

•P<.05 °P<.01 °°P<.005 °°°P<.001

* Reverse Scored

exposure, and there is a predisposition to stay with the organization: both constitute evidence for cognitive dissonance and a subsequently positive evaluation of the chosen job whether or not expectations are fulfilled. It will be remembered that post-choice dissonance has only short-lived effects however, and the further factor of choice autonomy is required for commitment to be sustained. Again these are precisely the conditions pertaining here: job alternatives are high, which together with the minimal previous company exposure and high tenure intention, conspires to produce positive effects on the dependent variables, especially organizational commitment.

A similar picture emerges when focusing on the external constraints aspect of job choice. It has already been noted that low external pressure from other contributors is associated with high rank preference (T=.017, p< .01). This dimension of autonomy is also found to correlate significantly with the level of pre-entry level of expectations (T=.117, p < .05). However, just as it was discovered that more job alternatives were not being associated with improved match, so lower external influence does not enhance match as might be anticipated: indeed there is a negative correlation with matched expectations (T=.-108, p < .05) and a positive correlation with mismatch (T=.124, p < .01). Thus the influence of external constraints on desire to stay and intended tenure reported earlier cannot be attributed even indirectly to the matching hypothesis. There seems to be no doubt that as with the case of alternatives the impact of external constraints on these dependent variables is due entirely to the greater sense of autonomy exercised in the original job choice; in this case freedom from the influence of family and friends.

How, then, can we explain the demonstrated association between rank and the job satisfaction measures? These measures ask the subject to evaluate different aspects of his job and its environment about six months after joining the company; in other words they tap the feelings of the individual about the content of his new work. Of the four job choice variables, the one that corresponds most closely with this is rank, since this dimension of job choice was intended to discover the presence of extrinsic basis for action. By asking the respondent to rank the chosen job against his original preferences the researcher discovers how much the job choice was made based on the respondent's own feelings for the job. It follows then that securing a job which was first - or at least high - in terms of personal preference constitutes strong evidence that the decision is based on an intrinsic basis, rather than being based on less preferable extrinsic constraints, and it is not surprising that this particular facet of choice autonomy leads to expressed satisfaction with the content and nature of the job. Number of alternatives, market pressure and the presence of other contributors are all factors which concern the circumstances rather than the substance of job choice and seem to relate less directly to the subsequent evaluation of job content.

Once again, there is a noticeable absence of association between rank preference and the expectations level variables: securing a highly ranked job might reasonably be expected to bring about a high match, but this is not the case (table 6.1). However high rank does correlate with plans to stay long-term (T=.126, p< .05) which has already been found to be a good indicator of future commitment as shown in table 7.2. Further, rank preference also correlates positively with length of time with the company (T=.142, p< .05), unlike alternatives and external constraints where this relationship is negative, and this is probably due to the high sandwich element of the 'with company' variable. In most cases their original rank preference would accord with their present employer on account of contractual obligation as much as personal choice, and so high rank and length of time with the company are naturally linked variables.

The relationships of perceived irrevocability with the other variables require some comment. As predicted by Salancik (1977) and demonstrated empirically by O'Reilly and Caldwell (1981), irrevocability in this research serves to enhance job satisfaction, in that preference for moving jobs diminishes (T=.-150, p < .005). However when crosstabulated with the other job choice variables, the association is negative, such that greater autonomy in the form of more alternatives and low market pressure is associated with low irrevocability because the greater range of job opportunities implies that the job choice is more easily revoked (1). On the face of it, this is logically consistent but the theory predicted that high, not low, irrevocability induces commitment, since post-action justification is not called for following a choice which is easily reversed anyway. It can be seen that the job choice set of variables pose an internal contradiction: while in the case of alternatives, market pressure, external constraints and rank preference, greater autonomy is hypothesised to lead to positive job responses, when referring to irrevocability it is proposed that greater constraint enhances job satisfaction and organizational commitment. The findings here are consistent with this: the fact that perceived irrevocability before entry correlates negatively with job alternatives and market pressure demonstrates that it taps a very different facet of job choice, and the fact that irrevocability also correlates with preference to move shows that it is nevertheless a legitimate dimension of job choice which has an influence on the individual's response to the job.

What conclusions can be drawn from this discussion of the differential effects of job choice autonomy upon job satisfaction and organizational commitment?

(1) In comparison with the expectations variables, their impact on the dependent variables is far more sporadic, probably because each is tapping a very different dimension of freedom of choice.

(2) A greater number of job alternatives at the time of choice enhances organizational commitment but not job satisfaction.

(3) Hypothesis four is confirmed: freedom from the external constraint of market pressure has no significant impact on job satisfaction and organizational commitment.

(4) Freedom from other contributors when choosing the job leads to greater organizational commitment but has no effect on job satisfaction.

(5) Greater autonomy in terms of securing a job of high personal preference enhances job satisfaction, but not organizational commitment.

(6) Perceived irrevocability correlates with one of the job satisfaction dimensions, but not with organizational commitment.

Thus, although the evidence is piece-meal rather than comprehensive, the relationships, where significant, are in the predicted direction, and when taken together they provide substantial support for the retrospective justification section of the research model.

THE CONTROL VARIABLES

In the literature review (chapters 2 and 3) the importance of not overlooking variables beyond the immediate scope of the job entry process was emphasised; for this reason a number of control variables were incorporated into the overall model as depicted in figure 4.3. Are these variables associated with the independent and dependent variables under consideration in this study, and if so what is the nature of this influence in terms of moderating or attenuating the relationships so far discovered in this chapter?

Tables 7.2 and 7.3 show the assocation between some of the relevant biographical and educational variables and a number of the independent variables. Since this subject data was measured at a nominal level the chi-squared statistic is used to establish significance, whereas table 7.2 shows associations between ordinal pre-entry controls and the independent variables, and these are summarised by the Kendall rank correlation coefficient.

Expectations. Neither father's occupation, nor type of secondary school, nor degree type and class have any apparent affect on the formation of realistic, or subsequently congruent, expectations. There is a fairly strong assocation between amount of prior contact with the company in terms of interviews and visits and the level of pre-entry expectations about the job and organization ($X^2 = 4.50$, p < .05, T=.171, p < .001). Linked with this the quality and quantity of job information before commencing employment is also significantly correlated with level (T=.178, p < .001; T=.152, p < .005 respectively). While these relationships suggest that level provides a useful measure of realistic expectations, the other findings arouse suspicions that this is not the case. One would expect, for instance, sandwich and especially sponsored students to exhibit greater accuracy in what they expect of employment, yet the associations between level and sandwich ($X^2 = 4.82$, p < .05) and sponsorship ($X^2 = 4.13$, p < .05) are negative; at the same time level is highly correlated with plans to stay long-term (T=.342, p < .001), which taps an individual's estimated future commitment to the company. Furthermore there is a notable absence of relationship between the expectations variable which measures discrepancy and any of these variables. This cluster of relationships suggest that contact with the company and its representatives have more to do with the conception of an inflated view about the future job than the development of down-to-earth expectations which experience proves to be accurate, and leads to the conclusion that level is not so much a measure of realism as optimism.

Job Choice. Again father's occupation, type of school and type of degree appear to have no constraining influence upon the graduate's freedom of choice. However the higher the class of degree the more competitive the labour market is perceived to be ($X^2 = 4.64$, p < .05), the reverse of what might be anticipated. Possibly highly qualified graduates set their

Table 7.3 - Association between biographical/educational controls and independent variables (X²)

	Father's Occupation	Secondary Education	Degree Type	Degree Class	Sandwich Training	Sponsor-Ship	General Wk Experience
EXPECTATIONS							
Discrepancy*	.33	1.91	2.45	.66	.36	1.88	1.29
Pre-entry level	.63	8.63	3.82	.01	4.84*	4.13*	.50
Match	-	-	-	-	101.53°°°	35.64°°°	8.98°°
Mismatch	-	-	-	-	25.91°°°	50.17°°°	7.73°°
JOB CHOICE							
Job Alternatives	1.42	5.36	2.94	1.24	2.08	.32	3.39
Market Pressure*	.01	1.42	4.95	4.64*	.36	5.09°	1.70
External Constraints	.66	5.24	2.75	.12	1.52	5.86°	.48
Rank Preference*	2.59	6.15	1.95	.08	1.06	5.67°	2.22
Irrevocability	.00	1.62	.96	1.05	.02	.70	1.37

*P<.05; °P<.02; °°P<.01; °°°P<.001

*Reverse Scored

career targets higher than those with more lowly qualifications who would settle for one of a more plentiful supply of mediocre jobs.

When plans to stay are long-term the freedom from market pressure is felt to be a greater (T=.192, $p < .001$); in other words there seems to be an assocation between autonomy and future commitment as posited by the retrospective justification hypothesis.

The fact that the four job choice variables tap very different facets of the decision process is borne out by these findings, particularly those relating to sponsorship. On the one hand, sponsored students see their job choice constrained by the influence of others because it is rooted in an early, parentally dominated career decision ($X^2 = 5.86$, $p < .02$). However in terms of pressure from the graduate labour market ($X^2 = 5.09$, $p < .02$) and personal preference as derived from rank ($X^2 = 5.67$, $p < .02$) the sponsored student sees himself as more autonomous than his non-sponsored counterpart who has all the competition of graduate recruitment to contend with.

There is a similarly varied relationship between previous work with the company and the job choice variables. Whereas, having worked six months or more with the employing organization is associated with freedom from market constraints – probably because employment was guaranteed – job choice is nevertheless constrained by few alternatives and the influence of others, which are also the two dimensions of autonomy that correlate significantly with subsequent organizational commitment.

We can conclude that for sandwich students, the advantages of having employment secure and not having to compete in the graduate labour market are largely offset by lack of alternatives at the time of graduation and external influence upon their original decision, even if the organization joined was, originally, a first or high preference.

This has implications for the relationships between job choice and the dependent variables, where one assertion was that low market pressure would lead to high satisfaction and commitment due to retrospective justification processes. While this may be the case, it has been found here that other circumstances pertaining to autonomy of choice, namely the number of job alternatives and the influence of other contributors, serve to constrain the decision and exert a negative influence on the dependent variables, irrespective of freedom from market pressures.

In the light of the pattern of relationships discussed above, it is probable that these are the key facets relating to autonomy of choice. In other words the relationship pivots not so much on the sandwich/non-sandwich split but more on whether that sandwich training was sponsored, and the amount of time it entailed working for the company prior to graduation.

The only biographical variable to have consistent impact on the dependent variables is father's occupation (table 7.4). The contingency table for these variables reveals that in terms of both job satisfaction and future commitment graduates from professional backgrounds respond more positively. Table 6.6 illustrates the effects of the education control variables which tend to have greater influence upon the dependent variables. For instance, type of degree is associated with weighted satisfaction ($X^2 = 8.05$, $p < .02$), and intended tenure ($X^2 = 6.12$, $p < .05$). Closer scrutiny of the crosstabulation of these variables shows that those studying engineering at university are relatively less satisfied than their science and social science contemporaries. Nevertheless the future commitment of engineering graduates compares favourably with science graduates (but not social science graduates, who are even more committed at this stage to their employers). This may be due to the vocational nature of engineering training in that despite poor job satisfaction they remain persistent in the pursuit of professional expertise which entails tenure with their employer (2).

The most striking set of relationships from table 7.5 is the negative association between sandwich training and the organizational commitment dimensions, all of which are significant except values commitment. Again the bivariate contingency tables reveal a fuller picture: the negative relationship is apparent between sandwich and sponsored students and all the dependent variables; but only in the case of sandwich students and general commitment are the variables significantly associated. Approaching two-thirds of non-sandwich students register high organizational commitment contrasting with a similar proportion of the sandwich sample who express low commitment to the organization; a parallel, but modified pattern is reflected in the sponsorship tables. One possible explanation is that greater exposure to industrial experience as a student decreases a graduate's commitment to the organization because he regards his industrial training as giving him greater marketable value: this perhaps inculcates a restlessness not yet applicable to his non-sandwich contemporaries who remain relatively committed to the job choice they have recently made.

Table 7.4 - Association between biographical controls and dependent variables (X2)

	age	marital status	nationality	sex	father's occupation
Discrepancy*	3.32	5.61°	.43	.48	2.50
Pre-entry level	2.73	2.79	1.39	.78	1.27
Match	4.93	1.28	1.34	.04	1.43
Mismatch	4.55	1.18	1.33	.73	2.07
Job Alternatives	1.28	3.68	3.52	.83	.54
Market Pressure*	3.07	3.53	.77	.14	8.04°
External Constraints	2.43	1.12	1.14	1.27	8.68°
Rank Preference*	2.06	1.12	1.14	.01	10.35°°°
Irrevocability	2.28	1.02	2.45	.64	2.00

$^{*}P < .05$ $^{o}P < .$ $^{oo}P < .01$ $^{ooo}P < .001$

* Reverse Scored

Nevertheless the autonomy of that job choice may well be the primary factor at work here: it was found that the negative relationship between previous work or company experience and the dependent variables was due - at least partially - to limited freedom of choice; naturally sandwich/sponsored students approximate very closely with those high on prior work experience and it is therefore likely that their poor commitment is also a consequence of constrained job choice.

Where the previous work experience was of general nature and not related to that of the company joined, the only impact on the dependent variables, is a positive correlation with job satisfaction (T=.131, p< .05). Also from table 7.5 it will be noted that when class of degree is high, that is a first or upper second, the expressed commitment to stay with the organization is low in terms of future tenure (X^2=6.12, p< .05, df2). As with relevant industrial experience, it is likely that an individual regards his good qualifications as enhancing career prospects which in fact diminishes his tenure commitment because he has the confidence to be looking elsewhere for a better job.

Work-related control variables

A number of interesting relationships emerge when work-related controls are correlated with the dependent variables (table 7.6). Apparently those graduates who are employed in the manufacturing sector are more likely to be satisfied than their counterparts in the public utilities, where high and low satisfaction is fairly even, or manufacturing construction, where twice the proportion express low rather than high satisfaction. Furthermore, engineers rather than those in R and D, Design, Accounting or Systems, are more likely to register overall satisfaction (X^2= 10.61, p < .05, 4df). This picture changes somewhat when measured in terms of organizational commitment; here graduates at BR and BGAS are significantly more likely to express long-term commitment: perhaps this bears out the image of public companies offering longer-term security but not necessarily the job rewards of the more competitive manufacturing sector.

Having prior contact with the company enhances overall satisfaction and job satisfaction, the correlation being significant in both cases (table 7.5), and the effect of this variable on organizational commitment is even more comprehensive, with significant correlation for each of the commitment dimensions. This finding accords with that of Ullman and Gutteridge (1974) who also discovered that greater knowledge of the company at the pre-entry stage, measured in

Table 7.5 - Correlation between educational controls and dependent variables (X2 & T)

	X2			T			
	degree type	sand-wich	spon-sored	class of degree	previous work	quantity of job info	quality of job info
overall satisfaction	.95	3.61	1.2	.009	.131°	.067	.065
prefer to move*	.68	1.34	3.00	.040	-.014	.032	.073
job satisfaction	4.08	2.22	.26	.058	.033	.011	.054
weighted satisfaction	8.05°	1.46	.09	.046	.023	-.057	.010
desire to stay	2.09	4.33•	.09	-.137	.052	.117•	.102
intended tenure*	6.12•	3.87°	2.23	.125•	-.093	-.129	.092
general comm't	2.76	7.20°°	3.62	.044	.070	.051	.104
comm't to stay	3.07	3.90•	3.62	.036	.024	.031	.139°
values comm't	1.10	3.74	2.51	.061	.077	.105•	.095•

•P<.05; °P<.02; °°P<.005; °°°P<.001

*Reverse Scored

terms of job-search, was associated with satisfaction with final job choice, with career progress and also with tenure with employer up to three years later. It seems that 'hard data' concerning the organization prior to entry has many positive effects and may well account for the securing of a better match because this preview affords the individual with more realistic expectations. On the other hand plans to stay is also a powerful pre-entry factor, having a unanimous correlation with all nine of the dependent variables, notably with organizational commitment; this strongly indicates the presence of retrospective justification.

Those who express the intention to stay long-term with their company before commencing employment also register high satisfaction in terms of preferring not to move (T=.139, p <.05) and are nearly twice as likely to register high rather than low general commitment (T=.232, p <.001) several months later. That is, the early statement of intent appears to have the binding effect on subsequent behaviours that the commitment theory postulates.

The degree of progress towards desired placement in the first job is also a very strong determinant of job satisfaction and organizational commitment. All four measures of job satisfaction correlate highly with this variable. Crosstabulations show that if placement is rated low, almost two-thirds of the sample also rate satisfaction low (X^2 =13.740, p < .001, T=.269, p < .001). This is consistent with the findings of other studies (eg. Mansfield 1971) and underlines the preoccupation, in the early months of employment, with securing a post which is desired, or at least being assured of this in the future. The 'plans to stay' aspects of organizational commitment are the most strongly associated with this variable, overall organizational commitment and values commitment less so.

It seems job satisfaction is weakly associated with the extent of social integration: when subjects see more of their work friends outside the workplace they are twice as likely to express high satisfaction (X^2 =5.920, p<.05. T=.125, p <.05). 'Friendly colleagues' was ranked overall sixth in the index of job importance items so it is not surprising to find social integration correlating - albeit mildly - with job satisfaction. There is no such association with organizational commitment, possibly because friendships with colleagues is seen as a function more of the job and the immediate workplace than of the organization as a whole. There was no assocation between the degree of performance feedback and the dependent variables.

Table 7.6 - Impact of work related controls upon job satisfaction and commitment

	X₂		Salary	T						
	Company	Function		Prior Contact With Co.	Plans to Stay	Progress to Placement	Time at Co.	Social Integration	Performance Feedback	Quality of Training
Discrepancy*	3.39	10.61•	5.27	.147°	.153°	.353°°°	-.139•	.112•	-.063	.315°°°
Pre-entry level	.74	1.61	.06	-.068	-.173°°	-.221°°°	.149°	-.065	-.037	-.218°°°
Match	5.88	3.00	1.68	.111°	.132•	.280°°°	-.168°	.111	-.067	.357°°°
Mismatch	4.75	4.07	.41	.078	.139•	.269°°°	-.143•	.125•	-.073	.355°°°
Job Alternatives	11.20°°	4.39	1.67	.144°	.416°°°	.165°°	-.031	.009	-.011	.265°°°
Market Pressure*	10.18°°	2.81	3.46	-.166°°	-.404°°°	-.171°°	.067	-.009	.011	-.215°°°
External Constraints	.32	2.20	1.03	.160°°	.232°°°	.010	-.107•	.068	-.042	.323°°°
Rank Preference*	.34	4.50	.03	.152°°	.240°°°	.108	-.139•	.092	-.053	.307°°°
Irrevocability	.88	2.00	3.05	.182°°°	.165°	.027	-.018	.012	-.012	.285°°°

•P<.05; °P<.02; °°P<.005; °°°P<.001

*Reverse Scored

The strongest and most consistent influence exerted by a control variable is that of the quality of training received which correlates significantly with all nine dependent variables. In many ways to ask subjects to rate their induction/training is to ask them to evaluate their jobs up to that point in terms of job satisfaction and the two questions are thus effectively measuring the same thing, and it is not surprising that they are highly correlated (T=.269, p< .001). However, a high estimation of induction and training also enhances organizational commitment in all five aspects, and therefore confirms that this aspect has a unique contribution to graduates' attitudes toward their job and organization.

The introduction of the variable that assesses the length of time spent with the company since graduation tests the extent to which satisfaction and commitment are simply a function of tenure. The fact that there is a significant correlation with several of the dependent measures (table 7.6) suggests that tenure does influence this dependent variable; specifically, the longer a subject has been with his employer the less likely he is to evince weighted satisfaction (T=.143, p< .05). The same effect arises with the general commitment and values commitment dimensions but this growing disaffection does not apparently affect detrimentally plans to stay with the organization.

Summary and conclusions

In summary, a number of control variables are found to have a direct impact upon the dependent variables; furthermore the significance of this impact seems to increase the closer they are in time proximity to the evaluation of job satisfaction and organizational commitment. Thus, of the biographical variables, only father's occupation has any consistent influence; when the effects of education/training are assessed, isolated relationships are discovered between degree type, class, sandwich training, pre-work exposure, and the dependent variables. With factors relating to immediate work experience, whether they be pre-entry like prior contact and tenure intention, or post-entry like progress toward placement and quality of induction, the influence of control variables upon job satisfaction and organizational commitment is far more systematic and significant. To what entent these control variables attenuate the associations between expectations/job choice and the dependent variables will now be discussed.

The effects of test variables

Having examined the impact of both independent and control variables upon the nine dependent variables in this study, it is pertinent to ask whether the hypothesised relationships persist even when controlling for a number of specified test variables. Using elaboration analysis it is possible to take a step beyond the bivariate tables described above by successively entering controls to observe their role in the basic relationship. This involves computing the chi-squared value for a contingency table between two variables and then to compare this with the equivalent value when controlled at two or more levels of a given test variable. This helps to explain the direction of the relationship and reveals the extent to which a control is responsible for the association. Obviously it would be superfluous to analyse all these variables in this way, however, the preceding analysis has already highlighted the key controls likely to have an effect on the hypotheses. In the following section the assocation between one dimension of each independent variable (expectations discrepancy, realism and freedom of choice) and a dependent variable is selected and interpreted at various levels of biographical, pre-entry and post-entry controls. Finally, expectations and job choice variables will be extracted and treated as control variables to assess their interrelation in the basic relationships.

The effect of expectations upon job satisfaction controlling for biographical, pre-entry and post-entry factors

This basic bivariate relationship is highly significant ($X^2 = 22.13$, $p < .001$) and table 7.7 gives a profile of the kind of graduate for whom matched expectations are particularly important. He is more likely to be from a professional background and educated at LEA or grammar secondary school. Almost exclusively he will be an engineering graduate with a high grade degree; presumably these factors combine to give the job seeker high hopes that his expectations of work will be fulfilled in the job, and this element becomes a vital ingredient of expressed job satisfaction.

The pre-entry variables vividly confirm the findings discussed earlier: those for whom discrepancy leads to dissatisfaction are made up almost entirely of non-sandwich, non-sponsored students and those low on industrial experience. This suggests that for those graduates who do have substantial prior work experience the content and matching of expectations is a less decisive issue because it has already been

Table 7.7 - Association between expectations discrepancy and job satisfaction, controlling for selected variables (X²)

Discrepancy x Weighted Satisfaction X^2 = 22.13^{ooo}

Father's Occupation	manual .07	skilled 6.58^{oo}	professional 11.61^{ooo}
Secondary Education	LEA 7.15	grammar 10.95^{ooo}	fee paying .14
degree type	engineering 23.58^{ooo}	science .02	soc. science etc .45
degree class	first 10.53^{oo}	2:1 6.79^{oo}	2:2 & lower 4.60$^{•}$

controlling for biographical variables

	Low	High
prior contact with co.	6.11^{o}	16.40^{ooo}
plans to stay	6.86^{oo}	2.80
sandwich	20.16^{ooo}(non san.)	3.46
sponsorship	19.98^{ooo}(non spon.)	1.89
general work experience	6.63^{o}	15.00^{ooo}

controlling for pre-entry variables

	Up to £6 th	£6-£7 th	£7th & Over
salary	24.09^{ooo}	2.16	.60

	Up to 6 months	Over 6 months
time at Co.	5.62^{o}	11.51^{ooo}

	Poor	Good
quality of training	8.59^{oo}	5.28^{o}

function	Syst .08	Acc .50	Eng'g 14.00^{ooo}	R&D .01	Other 1.21

	Poor	Good
progress to placement	5.21^{o}	11.81^{ooo}

controlling for post-entry variables

$^{•}P<.05$; $^{o}P<.02$; $^{oo}P<.$$^{ooo}P<.001$

encountered, and perhaps it is the circumstances of job choice that have become the more salient. In contrast those who have had a high amount of prior contact with the company in the form of interviews and visits, and also extensive work experience of a general unrelated nature, have had the opportunity to develop some definite expectations of their future workplace, which are as yet untested: hence the fulfillment or otherwise of these has a direct impact on job satisfaction.

Is the discrepancy/satisfaction relationship affected by post-entry factors? Training and placement were found to have significant direct impact on the dependent variables, but table 7.7 shows that when introduced as controls their influence is fairly ambivalent. Again, those working in the engineering function are most concerned about matched expectations. This also appears to gain in significance as time with the company passes, undoubtedly as tolerance of mismatches diminishes. Finally it is those with low rather than high salary levels who view the degree of match as instrumental to their satisfaction. O'Reilly and Caldwell (1980) found in their study of MBA graduates an unanticipated correlation between job satisfaction and choosing a job for its high salary. The converse corollary of this is that without the extrinsic benefit of a relatively good salary, graduates look to other features for their fulfilment, and matched expectations provides just this.

Table 7.8 displays the impact of biographical and pre-entry controls upon the level of expectations/organizational commitment relationship which originally had a chi-squared value of 8.59 (p <.01) (3). The pattern for biographical variables is broadly similar to that for congruent expectations above. The influence of expectations upon commitment is particularly important for those having little or no prior work experience, whether that be relevant to subsequent employment or of a general nature. This trend is not so dramatic as with the discrepancy dimension of expectations, but is nevertheless evident. Again this is probably due to the decreased salience of work expectations for those already familiar with the world of work. The relationship between level and organizational commitment is also stronger the longer the graduate intends to stay with the company; this is not surprising since the influence of this variable upon commitment has already been observed.

Table 7.8 - Association between level of expectations and organizational commitment controlling for selected variables(X2)

Pre-entry level x general commitment $X^2 = 8.59^{oo}$

		manual	skilled	professional
	father's occuation	.88	.63	3.86[*]
controlling				
for	secondary education	LEA 6.16°	grammar 6.54°	fee-paying .67
biographical				
variables	degree type	engin'g 3.57	science 3.18	soc-science etc .23
	degree class	first 3.91°	2:1 .00	2:2 & lower 9.36[oo]

		Low	High
controlling	prior contact with co	3.35	2.18
for	plans to stay	.27	5.02°
pre-entry	sandwich	2.40(non san.)	2.75
variables	sponsorship	5.74°(non spon.)	.13
	general work experience	9.41[oo]	.55

[*]P < .05

°P < .02

[oo]P < .001

The effects of expectations upon dependent variables controlling for autonomy of choice

One of the unique features of the research model developed in chapter four, is the amalgamation of both retrospective and matching theories in the explanation of early job behaviours. Table 7.9 provides some further empirical corroboration for this: it can be seen that the strong association between expectations discrepancy and weighted satisfaction which is 22.13 (p < .001), persists even when controlling for each of the freedom of choice variables; however for each dimension (except rank preference) greater autonomy is associated with enhanced job satisfaction. In other words, the matching hypothesis is confirmed, with a positive job response particularly accruing to those who also choose their job without external constraint, which also supports the retrospective argument (4).

The relationship between the expectations variables which tap realism (in this case prior industrial experience) and general commitment is significantly negative (X^2=7.13, p < .01), and it is interesting to note that the direction of this relationship is such that a high degree of expectations' accuracy leads to lower commitment to the company especially when the number of alternatives chosen from was low (X^2=8.13, p < .01) and freedom from external contributors was perceived as low. (See table 7.11). Thus, we find that the negative association between realism and commitment, which contradicts the matching hypothesis, can be largely attributed to the presence of a third factor, autonomy of choice. Because of this, notably where the number of job offers is low, there is no need for the graduate to employ self-justifying retrospective strategies.

The effects of job choice upon dependent variables controlling for expectations

Only one of the relationships between job choice and the dependent variables is significant according to the chi-squared measure of association: having a high number of job alternatives is positively related to the desire to stay with the company n the long-term (X^2=4.07, p < .05), a finding which supports the retrospective justification argument. However the introduction of weighted discrepancy as a test variable to this basic relationship reveals that when matched expectations are high (weighted discrepancy being low) the chi-squared value is 5.23 (p < .02), yet when the match is poor the association is minimal (X^2=.10). Once again this is evidence

Table 7.9 - Association between expectations discrepancy and job satisfaction, controlling for the job choice factors (X2)

Discrepancy x Weighted Satisfaction X^2 = 22.13$^{\circ\circ\circ}$

	low choice	high choice
Job alternatives	5.84°	16.30$^{\circ\circ\circ}$
Market pressure	9.25$^{\circ\circ}$	12.40$^{\circ\circ\circ}$
External constraints	5.10°	15.36$^{\circ\circ\circ}$
Rank preference	10.89$^{\circ\circ\circ}$	6.40°

•P<.05; °P<.01; °°P<.005; °°°P<.001

Table 7.10 - Association between previous, related work experience and organizational commitment, controlling for the job choice factors (X2)

Industrial experience x general commitment X^2 = 7.32$^{\circ\circ}$

	low choice	high choice
Job alternatives	8.13$^{\circ\circ}$	.46
Market pressure	3.10	3.28
External constraints	3.43	3.15
Rank preference	1.53	2.85

•P<.05; °P<.02 °°P<.01; °°°P<.001

of the prospective and retrospective hypotheses reinforcing
each other: in this instance the positive effects of job
choice autonomy are accentuated when there is also low
discrepancy of expectations.

The interrelation of job choice and expectations and their
effects on dependent variables

One of the assertions arising from the model is that the
prospective argument holds so long as the outcome of the job
choice is perceived as positive by the subject; if this is not
the case it is likely that retrospective self-justifying
strategies will be called into play. So far in the analysis
of results, the independent and combined influence of the job
choice and expectations variables upon the dependent variables
have been tested, and in several cases established; but
whether, and under what circumstances, the retrospective
hypothesis supersedes that of the more rational explanation is
not yet clear. Although this is an intricate process to test,
the following framework was set up on order to discover, at a
simplified level, the interrelated effect of choice and match
upon satisfaction and commitment, which would then suggest the
most plausible explanation (figure 7.1).

Four new variables were computed representing the degree of
match for each of the job choice dimensions, which had
previously registered significant relationships with the
dependent variables. Thus, for instance, the variable testing
number of alternatives broke subjects into one of four
possible categories and classified them as those having high
choice with either high or poor match, and those having low
job choice with either high or poor match (5). The prevailing
pattern that emerges from the contingency tables is as
follows: when subjects secure a high match of expectations job
satisfaction is also invariably rated more highly too; however
this trend is intensified when the individual perceived
himself to have had highly autonomous job choice (outcome (3)
in figure 7.1). For example, while 70% of those with high
match/low choice on the market pressure variable register high
job satisfaction, 87.5% of those with high match and high job
choice are highly satisfied. What happens when a subject
rates the degree of matched expectations as low? Not
surprisingly, job satisfaction is unanimously lower also, but
this relationship is more - not less - marked for those who
also exercised greater freedom of job choice (outcome 8); such
that on the market pressure variable again, 64% of those with
low match/low choice are found to be dissatisfied, compared
with 92% of those with low match but high choice. These
patterns are reflected broadly in the tables where

	Outcome	Likely explanation
	high j/s; o/c	- Match the primary factor, thus RATIONAL
Low choice		
	low j/s; o/c	- Probably RETROSPECTIVE. Despite high match, low autonomy of choice does not call for self-justification
High match		
	high j/s; o/c	- Either because high match (RATIONAL), and/or high choice calls for justification (RETROSPECTIVE)
High choice		
	low j/s; o/c	- Factor(s) other than choice or match since neither have predicted impact.
	high j/s; o/c	
Low choice		
	low j/s; o/c	- Either RATIONAL or RETROSPECTIVE
Low Match	high j/s; o/c	- Definitely RETROSPECTIVE despite low match, high choice calls for self-justification
High choice		
	low j/s; o/c	- Definitely RATIONAL because match the primary factor

j/s job satisfaction
o/c organizational commitment

Figure 7.1: <u>A framework for assessing the interrelated effects of choice and match upon satisfaction and commitment.</u>

organizational commitment is the dependent variable.

In short, matched expectations definitely determine job satisfaction and organizational commitment. If the good match was preceded by an autonomous job choice this increases the graduate's sense of satisfaction: not only has the job turned out well but in addition it was largely his own doing! However if the organization fails to meet his pre-entry expectations, <u>particularly</u> if the job was freely chosen, job satisfaction is rated low. In other words the matching hypothesis seems to be the dominant factor, with job choice autonomy serving to intensify the relationship either positively of negatively. This conclusion confirms retrospective justification theory, but only up to a point: it seems that a basic level of matched expectations are necessary for the new employee's sense of satisfaction and while greater autonomy of choice will enhance this positive job response, if experience of the job falls below this threshold requirement, no amount of autonomy will compensate in 'binding' the individual to his freely chosen course of action (as predicted by commitment theorists); indeed, the more autonomous the original decision the more damaging, it appears, the mismatch becomes.

How does this mesh with earlier findings? Naturally the findings of the congruent expectations hypotheses concur because the focus of these variables is the influence of match on the dependent variables regardless of autonomy. In the case of realistic expectations, graduates high on previous work or experience with the company were found to have low commitment and, to a lesser extent, low job satisfaction; and this was due not so much to expectations, where no significant associations emerged, as to job choice which was constrained. Secondly those with a high level of pre-entry expectations were found to have high job satisfaction and commitment, which was attributed to the associated high autonomy of choice, outweighing the effect of the poor match experienced by these graduates. If we are to be consistent this statement should now be revised: it appears unlikely from this analysis of the newly computed variables that freedom of choice, no matter how highly perceived, can actually reverse the effect of poorly matched expectations. Hence it must be assumed that the discrepancy of these subjects' high level expectations was not so great as to take them below the critical threshold beyond which freedom of choice ceases to have its positive effect: so these subjects would be located mainly in the high choice/high satisfaction cells of the contingency tables. Finally, in relation to the job choice variables themselves: for those that correlated with the dependent variables, that is alternatives, external constraints and rank preference, no associations were registered with expectations discrepancy. Hence it is probable that those graduates who exercised greater autonomy in their job choice, which resulted in high satisfaction and commitment, also experienced the required degree of matched expectations. These subjects then constitute those high proportions found in the high match, high choice/high satisfaction, high commitment cells.

NOTES

(1) Indeed, personal contact with a number of employers has confirmed the common practice of graduates apparently "accepting" more than one job offer and then backing down from all but one at a fairly late stage in the selection process.

(2) Qualifying for membership of one or other of the Engineering Institutes, for instance, would require consistent tenure with one employer.

(3) Unlike discrepancy, the variable 'level' is derived from pre-entry data alone hence assessing the impact of post-entry controls upon its relationship with organizational commitment would constitute retrospective imputation of meaning which is invalid.

(4) Why should the reverse hold true for RANK? Or why should the proportion of those for whom good match is associated with high job satisfaction be greater for those who secured a job of a lower personal preference? One can only suppose that not attaining a highly preferred job brought about a lowering of pre-entry expectations which resulted in greater realism and matching: the consequence being enhanced satisfaction.

8 Graduate opinion

The final section of the second questionnaire asks subjects about their experience of entry and induction to full-time employment, inviting an open-ended response. The three questions are related: the first asking whether any unanticipated surprises have been encountered in the new job, the second prompts the individual to recall the most significant events of the transition period and finally a carte blanche is given for the graduate to make any recommendations that might improve the integration of graduates into industry. It was hoped that this unstructured format would serve to amplify and add a qualititive dimension to the previous fixed-choice data. In fact, the majority of respondents did take this opportunity to make an uninhibited, and often extensive, assessment of their personal experience; some of the key trends arising from these comments are recorded below.

UNANTICIPATED SURPRISES

Just over one quarter (27%) registered unanticipated surprises. The vast majority being negative, but seven referred to situations where experience exceeded expectations, which demonstrates that organizational reality is not always disenchanting. Surprise elements covered a wide range of job aspects. Out of four who mentioned their induction and training, three were positive, impressed by the rotations and the flexibility of the programme and another by

the encouragement to study for an MSc. However two were
placed in jobs or departments different to that expected and
another was disappointed by a poor report given on him at a
six-month appraisal.

In relation to the work itself, a number were surprised by the
lack of pace and pressure in their jobs. While this is
possibly a function of graduate traineeship, these comments
were often linked with others concerning the backwardness of
company technology: for instance one entrant with a major
electronics company notes 'The work is very slow, considering
we are meant to be in a fast-moving industry'. Other
evaluations of the work itself were also negative; in
particular the routine nature of tasks, low responsibility and
irrelevant tasks were mentioned as being worse than expected.
However most comments in this section on surprise were
reserved for the wider, organizational climate. For instance
the sheer size of the organization, poor cooperation between
departments, inefficient administration and policy decisions
made with insufficient information were singled out for
special mention, as were employee attitudes in the form of
'widespread complacency', 'bloody-minded and unmotivated
workforce' and 'politicking and backstabbing'. One element of
surprise concerned major redundancies (16% of the workforce in
one organization were laid off at the Christmas following
graduate induction) and, naturally, this caused four graduates
from this company to register insecurity concerning the
future.

As might be anticipated non-sandwich graduates registered
surprise far more frequently than their sandwich counterparts,
and most were of a negative nature. The vast majority of
sandwich trained employees indicated that they had experienced
no unexpected surprises in their new work situation; clearly
their prior exposure to the company or work experience with a
related organization had provided them with a more complete
picture of what to expect of full-time employment.

SIGNIFICANT EVENTS

Events specified by subjects as either helping or hindering
their transition to employment covered a wide range of
aspects, but they fall broadly into four categories: those
concerned with the nature of the job, relationships within the
workplace, the quality of induction and training, and the
wider organizational climate. For the first three of these
areas graduates generally described events, people and
situations which were positively significant; whether this is
because they chose not to recall negative experiences is

134

difficult to assess. However, comments concerning the organization on a macro level were almost exclusively negative. Both in terms of proportion and direction there was very little difference between sandwich and non-sandwich respondents over these four areas.

Twelve graduates recalled favourable opportunities in their early work experience to take on jobs which entailed working under pressure, being responsible for others or just 'being thrown in at the deep end', and the sense of satisfaction and pride that ensued from completion of the task - even though mistakes had been incurred on some occasions. No less than 38 separate comments were made concerning relationships, either with the immediate superior (16) or with colleagues in the department (22): consistently respondents described social occasions where they were able to have an informal conversation with their boss, or quiz ex-graduates on their experience to date in the company, as being significantly valuable in helping them to settle into their jobs. In contrast four graduates highlighted a poor relationship with their superior as being a particular hindrance. It seems that the friendliness and helpfulness of colleagues is a factor which cannot be underestimated if the integration of graduate entrants is to be successful, with a major part of the responsibility falling on the graduate's manager.

Organizations differ ih their approach to graduate induction. Some have special graduate training schemes lasting for up to two years which are designed to expose newcomers to the whole scope of the company's activities; others place their graduates almost immediately into a job and expect them to absorb the wider aspects as they go along. Almost a third of the total sample (42) referred to their induction and/or training as having a significant impact upon their transition to employment. The consensus of opinion being that short induction to the company in a global way is preferable, lasting no more than a few weeks, followed by a definite assignment to a job with responsibility and relevance to future career, as against a mundane clerical job or training by passive observation. This quotation from a sandwich entrant to BGAS usefully summarises the view: 'the training course I am on is one week here, there and everywhere. I am not in one location long enough to do a job fully and hence I appear to be viewed by people who do the job as a "fly by night" management trainee'.

This also serves to introduce the fourth dimension of significant events: those relating to the organization as a whole and specifically the general attitude of employees to graduates. A number of respondents commented on the resentment expressed towards them by non-graduate colleagues and even bosses. For instance one female graduate described her discomfort at receiving perks (like a longer lunch-break) and a higher salary than those she was working with, including her superior. Other aspects of the organization not rated favourably were the 'amount of red tape for getting things done', minimal vertical communication, poor quality management and uncertainty concerning future prospects (again this latter comment was linked to a specific redundancy situation). Overall, of the 11 organizational events or situations that were recalled as significant, 10 were negative in nature.

IMPROVEMENT OF GRADUATE INTEGRATION

How can the integration of graduates into industry be improved? Most respondents voiced opinions on this subject and although the changes suggested reflect the kind of significant events and surprises already encountered, and recorded above, a number of new ideas emerged in this section.

Naturally, the university, the careers service, the employer and the individual each have a responsibility in this matching of individual needs and skills to employer requirements and opportunities. Taking these in turn, the prevailing opinion concerning university courses, from sandwich and non-sandwich graduates alike, was that they should be more practical and industry-orientated; suggestions here were for more lecturers with industrial experience, courses which included discussion of 'the processes, terminology and background theory of industry', which were less academic and more geared to, for instance, the 'laws, practices and procedures of civil engineering', and a number put forward the idea of industrial tutors at university who could talk to these issues. Linked with this was the argument that the careers service could do a better job in preparing candidates for the practicalities of working in industry by arranging more liaison with local employers and the engineering institutions.
Criticism of the company's part in the integration process fell into two broad areas: recruitment and induction. Of the 11 who mentioned recruitment and selection, the unanimous verdict was that employers should avoid over-selling themselves and provide, instead, situations where a frank and unpressured interchange could take place between employer and candidate. Apart from improved interviewing and more realistic exposure of the company's activities via university visits and brochures, the idea was put forward for company visits other than at the time of interview for prospective employees when neither side is trying to impress. As one

136

disenchanted graduate put it, companies should 'avoid cavalier recruitment into essentially low-key jobs that get represented as something else'. Comments concerning induction underline those made earlier: there was a strong preference for shorter induction programmmes, either at the very start or after a few weeks with the company, and then the opportunity to start on a specific job. The 15 or so who mentioned this first job called for more responsibility, shorter deadlines, the chance to use skills and abilities and work with more experienced colleagues rather than alone and with a boss who was encouraging and aware of the graduate's background. A number of other ideas emerged where the initiative for improvement lay with not just one of the above parties, and not least, with the individual. Sandwich courses, or work placements in industry during vacations was a suggestion most popular with sandwich students themselves, although mentioned by non-sandwich graduates. Also, having the opportunity to meet with ex-graduates with a year or two of industrial experience was seen as another way or preparing for full-time employment. Finally, attitudes of and towards graduates were singled out as an important element of integration, and perhaps significantly, all these comments came from those with sandwich training. Graduates, it was stated, should 'remember they are on the bottom rung', and realise that 'it is up to them to fit into the organization'. For the employers, they 'should not set graduates up on pedestals' and 'should stop regarding graduates as special since this causes alienation from others'.

SUMMARY

While the above responses to the open-ended questions have only an indirect bearing on the research hypotheses under examination, they do help to amplify and elaborate earlier quantitative findings, particularly those in relation to the matching model. The degree of surprise is, for example, substantially less for those with realistic expectations, and discrepancies - where they occur - relate primarily to the lack of pace, variety and responsibility in initial work/training placements or to the wider ethos of the organization where apathy, inefficiency and resentment toward graduates are particularly noted. The poignancy of this unexpected mismatch is heightened by the 'glossy' picture typically conveyed by the company at the recruitment stage.
On the positive side, where colleagues and superiors have been helpful, friendly and sympathetic, and also where the organization assisted with initial accommodation (mentioned by 12 different subjects) the assessment is very favourable, underlining the importance of the 'personal touch' in graduate

induction. This is illustrated by this comment from a BP sandwich graduate: 'I went through the trauma of settling into industry five years ago when I joined my sponsoring company ... even then the most significant lubricant for the transition was being given accommodation for the first few weeks until something more permanent was found'.

Overall then organizational reality does commonly produce a serious element of surprise, particularly for the non-sandwich graduate, but this is not necessarily negative. There is much critism of poorly planned and undemanding training programmes and initial placements, but also approval of unanticipated helpfulness amongst colleagues. Significantly most mentions for improving integration concern the gaining of first-hand work experience prior to employment, either through sandwich schemes or vacation work; and it is those who have had sandwich training who suggest that the onus for industrial adjustment lies as much with the individual, as with the university or employer.

9 Conclusion

The research model tests a number of relationships. These concern the effects of congruency of expectations, realism of pre-entry expectations, and the degree of job choice autonomy upon the dependent variables, job satisfaction and organizational commitment. These are summarised in figure 9.1, together with the model in figure 9.2. In addition the influence of variables reflecting a subject's biographical, educational and work experience background are also assessed. Having discussed in detail the direction, significance and possible explanation of these inter-relationships, and having recorded the open-ended responses, which add a qualitative dimension to the results, it is now possible to draw together the various threads of the argument and relate the findings first back to the research model and accompanying hypotheses, then to the literature from which the study was launched and third to the practical implications which arise for all parties involved in graduate integration.

THE RESEARCH FINDINGS AND THE MODEL

The expectations hypotheses

Focusing on the top half of the research model (figure 9.2) it was predicted that when a graduate's experience of the job and organization proved to be congruent with what he anticipated, and/or when the content of his pre-entry expectations was

JOB/WORK EXPECTATIONS

1. Realism of expectations
       Level of pre-entry expectations
       Related work experience
       Prior work experience with the company

2. Congruency of expectations
       Matched expectations
       Mismatch between expectations and experience
       Mismatch, weighted according to relative importance
          of job items

CIRCUMSTANCES OF JOB CHOICE

3. Autonomy
       Number of job alternatives
       Degree of market pressure
       Degree of external influence upon decision
       Personal preference ranking of job chosen

4. Revocability
       Perceived revocability of changing jobs

Figure 9.1 <u>A summary of the independent variables</u>

realistic then he would subsequently evaluate his job favourably and be committed to his new employer. In the course of testing these variables it emerged that prior industrial experience and time spent previously with the company were reliable indicators of this pre-entry realism, while the original variable, intended to measure this, in fact tapped a third facet of expectations: the degree of pre-entry optimism. Figure 9.3 depicts in simplified form the effects of these three strands of expectations upon job satisfaction and organizational commitment.

Congruent expectations measured by the variables match, mismatch and discrepancy have the effect of increasing satisfaction and commitment. It can be seen that this congruency (which, naturally, is assessed after entry) is associated with a low level of expectations; indeed, in that the level of pre-entry expectations precedes congruency chronologically it is likely that this lack of optimism actually contributes to this matching. Congruency is also associated with low autonomy of choice, which might reasonably be expected to bring about greater - not less - discrepancy; however it has been argued that this limited choice prompts the graduate to lower his expectations realising that he may have to settle for something less than ideal because of constraints upon him; an interpretation which certainly ties in with the observation of diminished optimism.

High realism is associated with high congruency because expectations which are accurate are more likely to be matched on the job; nevertheless it is the congruency rather than the realism that is the key ingredient as can be seen from figure 9.3 (2), where realistic expectations correlate negatively with the dependent variables. The explanation for this unanticipated finding is that the low freedom of choice which accompanies the high realism is responsible for the negative impact on satisfaction and organizational commitment; in other words, for those with extensive sandwich and sponsorship experience the importance of matched expectations is superseded by other factors, one of which appears to be the amount of autonomy exercised in the obtaining of the job.

This attenuation caused by job choice variables is also evident in the positive relationship between level of expectations and the dependent variables which appears to be determined by the association of level with freedom from external influence and high tenure commitment prior to entry, rather than congruency or realism, both of which are low. Thus all the expectations variables have significant effects upon satisfaction and commitment, but not always in the

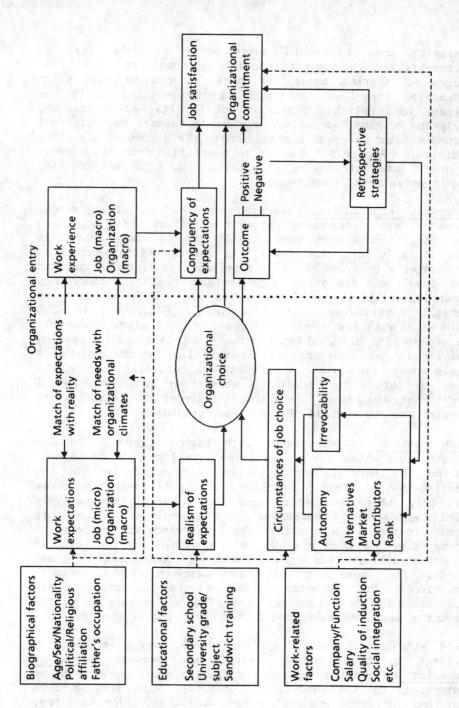

Figure 9.2 The research model

142

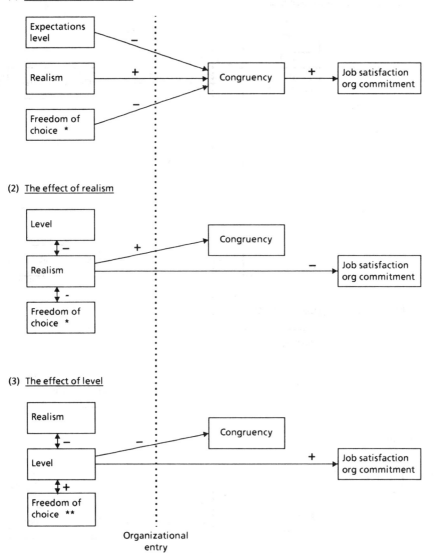

(1) The effect of congruency

Expectations level — Congruency
Realism + Congruency
Freedom of choice * — Congruency
Congruency + Job satisfaction org commitment

(2) The effect of realism

Level
— Realism
Realism + Congruency
Realism — Job satisfaction org commitment
- Freedom of choice *

(3) The effect of level

Realism
— Level
Level — Congruency
Level + Job satisfaction org commitment
+ Freedom of choice **

Organizational entry

*   Job alternatives and external constraints
** External constraints and plans to stay

Figure 9.3   A summary of the effects of expectations on satisfaction and commitment

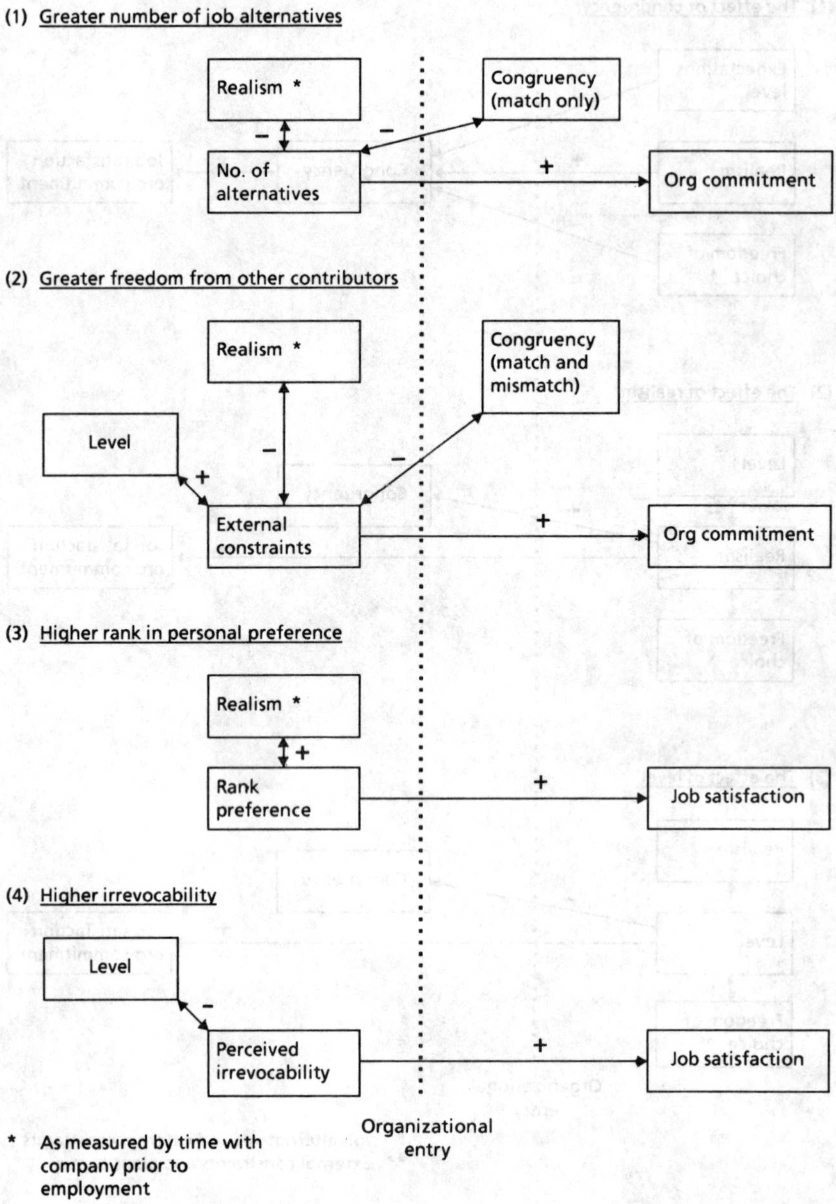

(1) Greater number of job alternatives

Realism *

Congruency (match only)

No. of alternatives

−

−

+

Org commitment

(2) Greater freedom from other contributors

Realism *

Congruency (match and mismatch)

Level

+

−

−

External constraints

+

Org commitment

(3) Higher rank in personal preference

Realism *

+

Rank preference

+

Job satisfaction

(4) Higher irrevocability

Level

−

Perceived irrevocability

+

Job satisfaction

Organizational entry

* As measured by time with company prior to employment

Figure 9.4   A summary of the effects of freedom of job choice on satisfaction and commitment

direction predicted, and this will be taken up shortly with reference to the literature.

The job choice hypotheses

The lower half of the research model highlights the circumstances of the job choice decision and the extent to which a graduate's autonomy in choosing his employer influences his subsequent job satisfaction and organizational commitment. Figure 9.4 illustrates the differential effects of four choice variables upon the dependent variables.

For both job alternatives and external pressure the association with congruent and realistic expectations is low: those who perceived themselves to have an autonomous job choice from a number of alternatives and free of external interference are also likely to be those committed to an employer upon graduation. Their lack of pre-graduation industrial experience also accounts for the low degree of expectations congruency, although this is not registered on the most sensitive weighted discrepancy variable, hence one concludes that the mismatch is not great for items important to the individual. Thus despite lack of realism and a low number of exact matches, the freedom of choice in terms of alternatives and external constraint is sufficient to create high organizational commitment, but not job satisfaction.

In contrast, when the job chosen also accords with high personal rank preference, job satisfaction results, as against organizational commitment, and in this case expectations are also realistic. Finally, a positive relationship between irrevocability of job choice and satisfaction is also apparent, at least with the job satisfaction variable which taps preference to move. The only significant association here with expectations is a negative one with level: it is reasonable to find a low level of expectations and anticipated difficulty of changing job linked in this way since both reflect a perceived competitiveness in the graduate labour market. Once again, it is established that all but one of the job choice factors influences one or other of the dependent variables and this time in the manner predicted.

The influence of control variables

The inclusion of a wide range of background control factors in the research model is vindicated in a number of areas. First of all, several have a direct impact upon the dependent variables under investigation. For instance, having a father in a professional, rather than in a skilled or manual, occupation enhances organizational commitment, and engineering students are more likely to express job satisfaction and future commitment than those of other university disciplines; and satisfactory progress towards placement, social integration and quality of induction/training are among the work-related factors which correlate highly with satisfaction and commitment.

Another way in which the control variables have proved valuable is in providing a fuller context for some of the main independent/dependent relationships. The variable measuring intended tenure at time one, for example, was found not only to have direct impact upon satisfaction and commitment but also to be strongly associated with level of expectations and freedom from market pressure. This helped to identify the optimistic nature of the level of expectations variable and further suggested that the statement of tenure intention prior to entry is an aspect of commitment in that it constitutes an action with a binding effect on subsequent behaviours. This becomes particularly apparent when used as a test variable: the tendency for congruency to result in satisfaction, and/or level of expectations to produce organizational commitment is far greater when this pre-entry tenure commitment is also high (tables 7.8 and 7.9).

Another variable feature of these tables is the influence of sandwich and sponsorship training upon the independent/dependent relationships: the likelihood of weighted discrepancy bringing about low satisfaction is almost exclusively accounted for by the non-sandwich/non-sponsored contingent of the sample on the one hand, and yet, on the other, those with general work experience and prior contact with the company in the form of visits and interviews also exhibit this relationship. The explanation being that for those with extensive industrial experience, factors other than matched expectations are integral to their expression of satisfaction, probably because the saliency of this issue has been eclipsed by another (and elsewhere this has been identified as job choice freedom). Whereas those whose exposure to the company's climates is limited to brief visits, backed up by work experience of a very general nature, develop some very definite but as yet untested views about what to expect of their future employment, and the fulfilment or otherwise of these is instrumental in determining their satisfaction. Thus the introduction of these and other control variables has enhanced understanding of the hypothesised relationships under investigation as well as demonstrating that some are worth testing as independent variables in their own right.

Overall assessment of the model

In summary, the findings have largely established that the research model is a valuable framework for assessing the impact of pre-entry factors upon subsequent satisfaction and commitment several months after entry. The results of t-test analysis revealed that with one exception all significant variances on mean scores for job choice and expectations discrepancies were accompanied by significant impact on the dependent variables, and there was no instance of a significant difference on a dependent variable not being associated with variance on one of the independent variables. The conclusion can be drawn that the job choice and expectation variables account for most if not all, of the variation in expressed job satisfaction and organizational commitment across all the companies in the sample. This, together with the recorded effect of a number of control variables, strongly suggests that the model is comprehensive.

A unique aspect of the model concerns the amalgamation of prospective rational and retrospective self-justifying theories, the argument being that both approaches are necessary for a total understanding of job entry processes. In several instances the efficacy of this research design has proved itself: in particular, explaining the unanticipated negative correlation between realism and the dependent variables, which contradicts 'matching theory', would have been impossible without accounting for the effects of job choice autonomy. Likewise the positive influence of pre-entry level of expectation upon job satisfaction and organizational commitment also confounded theoretical predictions, but again this relationship was better understood when the high association with freedom of choice, as well as with the control variables tapping sandwich training and sponsorship was discovered. This led to the deduction that level of expectations represented a picture of pre-entry job ideals (based usually on scant information) rather than an objective measure of informed realism.

So the explanatory power of the model appears to be adequate. This is not to say that all the hypothesised relationships were confirmed. A number were not, and some were significantly negative as noted in chapters six and seven, but in almost every case (the market pressure dimension of job choice being the only exception) the independent variables were significantly correlated with some or all of the job satisfaction and organizational commitment variables. In each case the internal relationships of the model were consistent and when taken together enabled a reasonable explanation to be made for the relationship in question. Furthermore, the longitudinal nature of research design and model, encapsulating as it does a six month transitional process means that the independent variables undeniably precede the registered impact on dependent variables; given also that the significance levels of such relationships and the attenuating effects of all relevant test variables have been ascertained it can be claimed that the model not only possesses explanatory but also predictive power.

One unconfirmed aspect concerns the retrospective strategies which in the model are said to be triggered by negative outcomes. In support of this it was demonstrated in figure 9.3 that congruency had a positive influence upon the dependent variables despite the associated low freedom of choice. When testing the interactive effects of matched expectations and freedom of choice upon the dependent variables in chapter seven it was discovered that a threshold appeared to be operating, whereby providing a certain degree of match (equivalent to a positive outcome) was obtained in the job, then if there was also freedom of job choice this would serve to enhance the positive impact on satisfaction and commitment. However, if such a threshold minimum was not achieved (that is, a negative outcome) then higher autonomy in choosing the job would not compensate but actually exacerbate the negative job responses. In other words, although low choice tends to lead to a high match (probably because limited job opportunities deflate optimism, increase realism and result in less discrepancy as shown in figure 9.3) when choice autonomy is high, graduates with a good match were more likely to express satisfaction and commitment.

While the model can accommodate this digression in its existing form it does call into question the assertion in retrospective literature that a poor outcome when freely chosen prompts self-justification which in turn increases commitment. In the light of the findings here we would have to argue that this mechanism would only operate providing a basic minimum of matched expectations had been attained in the new job, which may nevertheless represent a relatively 'negative' outcome in the eyes of the graduate. Below this threshold, whether retrospective reasoning was engaged by the entrant or not, the eventual impact on dependent variables would be a negative one; indeed the more autonomous the job choice the more negative the job response.

THE RESEARCH FINDINGS AND THE LITERATURE

The expectations hypotheses

The need to differentiate between the separately significant effects of initial and disconfirmed expectations has already been made (Oliver 1977; Louis 1980). It was for this reason that the research design adopted here took independent measurements of pre-entry realism and post-entry congruency of expectations and correlated these with subsequent job response.

Our first hypothesis relating to the strand of theory known as 'unmet expectations' was explicitly tested and confirmed in this research. A number of authors, including Ross and Zander (1957), Katzell (1968) and Dunette, Arvey and Banas (1973) have conducted studies whereby the difference between what newcomers expected of their work/training situation and what they actually encountered was shown to correlate with the dependent variables. Apparently this disconfirmation of expectations constitutes a broken promise in the view of the entrant resulting in dissatisfaction and decreased commitment to the company. A common methodological failing of these studies is that the data collection takes place only <u>after</u> the entry of subjects into their respective organizations and very often at only one point in time. This weakness was rectified here by a longitudinal treatment which covered a pre-entry, post-entry transition period, and congruent expectations were still found to have the predicted effect. In relation to the other approach to expectations, which focuses on realism prior to entry, the inflated nature of pre-entry expectations found by Ward and Athos (1972), partly attributable to the mutual selling situation of graduate selection (Porter, Lawler and Hackman 1975) and partly resulting from post-choice dissonance (Vroom and Deci 1971; Lawler, Kuleck, Rhode and Sorenson 1975), was definitely established here also, but the detrimental effects of such unfounded optimism as tested in hypothesis two was not supported by the findings. In fact, those with most familiarity about the job and organization they were joining were those registering least satisfaction and commitment six months later. While realism here was measured according to the amount and relevance of previous industrial experience, the traditional method for operationalising pre-entry realism in the literature has been the experimental use of a realistic job preview (RJP): the postulation being the RJPs decrease newcomers' initial expections, lower expectations are more likely to be met, and met expectations lead to satisfaction, which in turn is inversely related to voluntary turnover.

The various linkages of this argument have been tested with

varying degrees of success.   That RJPs decrease expectations was found to be the case in two experiments (see Wanous 1973) and was also substantiated in this research where the equivalent measure of realism was inversely related to level of expectations. Furthermore realistic expectations were also found to associate with congruent or met expectations (see figure 9.4).   However, the proposed argument then flounders, for despite being lower and less discrepant the observed effects of realistic expectations on satisfaction and commitment is negative.   This evidence in fact confirms that of Ilgen and Dugoni (1981) who, in a systematic examination of the effects of RJPs, found the one unsupported relationship to be that between lowered expectation and satisfaction.   The inadequacies of the RJP as a means of assessing realism have already been discussed and pointed out by others (Reilly, Tenopyr and Sperling 1979; Dugoni and Ilgen 1981), and it was for this reason that prior, relevant industrial experience was substituted as a realism measure.   The efficacy of this instrument appears well proven, and similar results emerge: pre-entry realism does not enhance satisfaction. However, the explanation for such an effect, counter intuitive as it is, was found to be lacking in the literature.   In the case of this research the explanation is to be found in the constrained job choice of the otherwise realistic graduates, leading to a negative job response, particularly in terms of commitment.   Unfortunately, since this dimension is almost exclusively peculiar to sandwich students, bound as many are to their employers, this deduction cannot be offered as general explanation of the relationship between the high realism and low satisfaction/low commitment.   What this finding does demonstrate, however, is that theories relying on prospective rationality alone may well overlook important aspects of the job entry process which provide a significant contribution to the determination of subsequent job attitudes. It is to these aspects that we now turn.

The Job Choice Hypotheses

The switch in emphasis from the content and realisation of work expectations, to the circumstances in which that job choice was taken, was first made in relation to graduate job entry by O'Reilly and Caldwell (1980), although the importance of constraining influences flowing from choice have been examined previously in the field by Staw (1974), who investigated the enrolment and tenure of cadets on a training programme, and experimentally by a number of researchers (for instance, Comer and Laird 1975; Lepper and Greene 1975; Mynatt and Sherman 1975; Folger, Rosenfeld and Hayes 1978). Arising from the theoretical work of Kiesler and Sakamura (1966) and

Kiesler (1971), Salancik in 1977 specified several conditions under which choice was likely to be particularly binding; it is these criteria that O'Reilly and Caldwell test in their longitudinal study of MBA graduates (1980; 1981).

Adapting the questions that O'Reilly and Caldwell used, to suit a UK graduate sample, three of the four hypotheses concerning autonomy of job choice were confirmed in this research: having more alternatives to choose from and greater freedom from other contributors enhanced organizational commitment, and attaining a job of high personal preference (also constituting high autonomy) had positive effects on job satisfaction, as with O'Reilly and Caldwell's sample. The effects of freedom from market constraint, tapping 'external demands for action', were not supported, and irrevocability had only an isolated impact on one dimension of job satisfaction. Thus with these exceptions the predictions of the post-action justification theory are borne out here, and the view that reality, in this case the assessment of a new job, is largely a retrospective construction of social and informational cues (Berger and Luckman 1966; Salancik and Pfeffer 1978) is also supported. Namely, in this research, a graduate's evaluation of his new job was significantly influenced by his re-assessment of the alternatives and outcomes open to him at the point of entry.

However it has been shown that the positive consequences of such self-justifying strategies will only operate above a certain threshold of matched expectations, and this finding has important implications for those who have recently argued for a retrospective rather than a prospective explanation of job behaviours (Pfeffer and Lawler 1980; Staw 1980; Salancik and Pfeffer 1978; O'Reilly and Caldwell 1981). If the consequences of action are negative then retrospective focusing takes place because there is dissonance (Staw 1980) (1). The present research findings suggest at least two refinements to this general theory: first even when experience is highly congruent with expectations (representing a positive outcome), freedom of choice serves to heighten the expressed satisfaction and commitment. Second, once an acceptable threshold of match is not attained, no amount of retrospective rationalising will retrieve positive responses to the job and organization. In short, the retrospective theory actively complements the prospective appproach when the match is high, compensates when congruency is lower though still apparent, but accentuates negative job attitudes once matched expectations fall below a basic minimum.

The Control Factors

A number of significant relationships between the control and dependent variables support the findings of the authors. For instance, the socio-economic composition of the research sample did not differ markedly from that of Kelsall's cohort 20 years previously, published in 1972, and it seems that the same effects of social differentiation upon career aspirations, choice and entry still prevail today.

In their evaluation of business studies and economics graduates who had trained at universities and polytechnics, Daniel and Pugh comment:

'One of the effects of placements is to give sandwich graduates the knowledge and confidence to look for higher levels of pay and promotion, while full-time graduates are still in the process of adjusting to first employment'. (1975, p.40)

and elsewhere they conclude that the value of industrial placements lies in the improved exposure to and appreciation of the life, work and poeple in industry and business, rather than in the supposed integration of formal education and practical experience, which they found to be poor. The implication that sandwich students are better informed prior to entry, yet more restless once employed is echoed in the research findings here, where somewhat surprisingly this realism of sandwich graduates translated into less, not more, satisfaction and commitment.

Several aspects of those first few months with the company emerged as having special influence on the dependent variables. The nature of the first work assignment, and the relationship with both superior and colleagues were consistently mentioned as having importance in the open-ended responses, and this underlines the validity of assertions by Schein (1978) and Van Maanen (1976) concerning early socialisation factors. Likewise the frequent reference to help given with initial accommodation, and the value of socialising with colleagues, in particular ex-graduates, gives credence to Louis' (1980) model of newcomer experience where such factors are crucial aspects of successful sub-cultural transition. Mansfield (1970; 1972) also found that degree of social contact outside work and progress towards placement in the early months correlated with subsequent graduate turnover, although 'ability to assess performance' did not. Once again, these findings were supported here where social integration and placement progress (but not performance feedback) significantly influenced the dependent variables.

Thus, the impact of many biographical, educational and work-related control factors predicted by the literature have been included in the analysis and found to be important elements of the overall entry process. In the light of these and the other research findings, what practical steps might be taken to improve the integration of graduates into full-time employment?

THE RESEARCH FINDINGS AND GRADUATE INTEGRATION

Arising from the quantitative and qualitative results of this study, several practical implications could be noted relating to key aspects of both undergraduate training and early work experience.

Recruitment, selection and undergraduate preparation

Finding job and organizational features to be as anticipated prior to entry is a vital ingredient of an individual's evaluation of his new work situation. Thus recruitment encounters where the applicant and company regard themselves in a mutual 'selling' situation do not facilitate the development of accurate expectations. Although there will inevitably be an element of surprise, both positive and negative, as the individual moves from one cultural setting to another (Louis 1980), unnecessary discrepancy could be diminished in a number of ways. Company information must be a faithful reflection of the organization's training, work climates and career paths. Opportunities for visits and discussion with prospective employers is already done, but this should be separate and removed from the pressures, no matter how subtle, of needing to impress (the involvement of ex-graduates would be especially valuable here). University courses should have a more explicit industrial orientation, if an objective of the course is vocational, including the use of lecturers with industrial experience, closer liaison with relevant professional institutes and some intensive pre-employment preparation in the final years. Alongside this, students should be encouraged to use some or all of their pre-university and vacation periods gaining first-hand experience relevant to their employment destination.

Sandwich Training

Somewhat paradoxically those with extensive industrial exposure, particularly with the company they subsequently joined, express low satisfaction and commitment. In these cases the realism of their work expectations has already become apparent to individuals, and the method of choosing their employer has become a more crucial issue. Frequently, sponsored students exercise little or no choice because they are contractually bound (morally or legally) to return to an organization, and the original choice was probably externally influenced by parents anyway. Of the 54 sandwich students in this sample, 25 were sponsored and more had prior work experience with the company they joined.

It has already been noted that empirical evaluation of sandwich training is limited to one study by Daniel and Pugh (1975). Based on the results of this and the present research findings, the primary benefit of sandwich training derives from the increased exposure to the everyday practicalities of industry and business: Daniel and Pugh found that the integration of these placements with university courses was usually ineffective. Furthermore it has been established that the obligation to return to a predetermined employer leads to low organizational commitment if not job satisfaction. Thus, for the relevant undergraduate faculties to encourage (and if necessary, help to arrange) industrial placements during the time spent at university, would seem to provide all the merits of such experience without the disadvantage of constraining the individual's choice of employment on graduation. Indeed, both graduate and employer might welcome the option of accepting or rejecting each other at this point.

Induction and Training

The findings concerning the early work experience conform to those traditionally uncovered in studies of organizational socialisation. In particular, employers should: limit their graduate induction to a few weeks at or near the commencement of employment and provide a placement relevant to the entrant's career path as soon as possible; the initial work task should ideally be a project working with older, more experienced colleagues, with closely controlled deadlines and carrying a degree of real responsibility; finally the newcomer's superior should be someone at least familiar with undergraduate training, if not a graduate himself, and committed to the development of such a resource.

While this longitudinal research represents an advance over previous studies which have typically relied on one data collection or post-entry data alone, or have utilised an entirely prospective or retrospective model to explain the behaviour of new employees, certain questions remain unresolved. For example, reference was made in the analysis of results to a threshold of matched expectations below which retrospective justification would cease to have its positive effects. It would be very interesting to demonstrate more lucidly the interrelation of rational and retrospective mechanisms as they affect job behaviours generally, but in particular, to be able to locate and quantify the crucial threshold more precisely. Another question concerns the duration of the impact of pre-entry factors upon satisfaction and commitment, and specifically the point at which such factors are eclipsed by other socialisation variables more closely related to the nature of the job and organization.

Finally a good many observations have been made concerning the respective merits and advantages of sandwich as against full-time training; generally speaking, sandwich students have more realistic expectations but they perceive their job choice to be more highly constrained, resulting in much lower commitment to their employer at about six months. Does this represent a temporary dip in commitment which is later compensated by the more extensive experience of industry? Are the relatively positive job attitudes of non-sandwich students sustained or does their response to the job follow that of their sandwich counterparts with the approriate time lag? Do the advantages and disadvantages of doing sandwich placements level out with those who do not have this experience, and if so at what point does this levelling out occur? The results of this study tentatively suggest some answers to these questions but longitudinal research of a longer duration is required before any definite conclusions can be drawn.

NOTES

(1) Staw adds another factor called "ego-defensiveness". Even if the outcomes of action are negative prospective focusing may still follow if the individual's ego-defensiveness is low.

Appendix:
the questionnaires

This questionnaire is strictly confidential, and the researcher guarantees that the identity of the respondent will not be disclosed to the employer.

Please answer all questions as candidly as possible. Where alternatives are given please circle (e.g. 3) the appropriate number.

1   Name _____

2   Home Address _____

    _____   Tel: _____

3   Address at which you can be contacted in 6 months (if available):

    _____

    _____   Tel: _____

4   Marital Status: 1. Married 2. Widowed
                     3. Single   4. Divorced
                     5. Separated

5   If you are married, how many children do you have _____

6   Do you plan to marry in the next 6 months?
    1. Yes   2. No

7   Age: 1. 20 or under 2. 21-25 years
          3. 26-30 years 4. Over 30

8   Country of Origin: 1. Britain 2. E.E.C.
        3. Commonwealth
        4. Other (Please state) _____

9   Sex: 1. Male 2. Female

10 What is, or was, your father's type of occupation?
    1. Unskilled   5. Skilled
    2. Armed Forces   6. Other self-employed
    3. Semi-skilled   7. Employer, Manager
    4. Non-manual   8. Professional

11   What was the type of secondary school at which
     you spent the most time?
     1. Secondary Modern   3. Grammar
     2. Comprehensive   4. Public

12   Under which category was your undergraduate
     degree?
     1. Engineering/Technology   3. Social Sciences
     2. Science   4. Arts

13   What was your class of degree?
     1. First   3. Lower Second
     2. Upper Second 4. Third   5. Other (Specify)

14   Have you accepted a job yet?   1. Yes   2. No

15   (a) Name of the company _____
     (b) Date of acceptance (month) _____
     (c) Number of interviews with the company

     _____
     (d) Number of visits to the company (other
         than interviews) _____
     (e) Starting date with the company (day,
         month and year) _____

16   How may suitable alternatives did you have to
     choose from when you accepted the job?

     _____

17   a) Do you see this job as:
        1. a "Stepping stone" to something else?
               or
        2. A career in itself?

     b) How long do you think you should remain
        in this company before moving on? _____
        years.

18   On the basis of what you already know about the
     job and organization you are joining, how
     accurate are the following descriptive
     statements? Please circle the appropriate number

           4   3   2   1   0
     A very accurate   A very inaccurate   Do not
     description   description   know at
                                              this
                                              stage

a) There are very good career 4 3 2 1 0
prospects in the company

b) Graduate entrants receive 4 3 2 1 0
individual training

c) Company policies are fair 4 3 2 1 0

d) Movement from one department 4 3 2 1 0
/location to another is fairly
easy

e) There is a relaxed friendly 4 3 2 1 0
atmosphere in the department

f) The well-being of people is 4 3 2 1 0
of prime importance to the
management

g) The job involves a wide range 4 3 2 1 0
of different activities

h) Compared to other companies the 4 3 2 1 0
salary is good

i) Working hours are flexible 4 3 2 1 0

j) The company offers a steady 4 3 2 1 0
employment for the forseeable
future

k) The working conditions are good 4 3 2 1 0

l) The job makes use of individual 4 3 2 1 0
abilities

m) There is opportunity for travel 4 3 2 1 0
in the job

n) The job provides a sense of 4 3 2 1 0
intellectual achievement

o) The work is interesting 4 3 2 1 0

p) The job gives a high amount of 4 3 2 1 0
responsibility

q) The job involves being in 4 3 2 1 0
charge of other people

r) Further professional training   4   3   2   1   0
   and education is encouraged

s) The job entails working under   4   3   2   1   0
   pressure

t) The recreational facilities   4   3   2   1   0
   provided by the company are
   of a high standard

In the following section answer questions (19) – (23) if you
are a Sandwich Graduate OR questions (24) – (25) if you are
not a Sandwich Graduate.

SANDWICH GRADUATES

19 Type of sandwich course (e.g. thick, thin)
   _____

20 Were you sponsored by a company for
   all/some of the time?
   1. Yes, Name of Company _____
   2. No

21 How much time did you spend in industrial
   placements? _____ months

22 How much of this time in industrial placements
   was spent with the company you are joining?
   _____ months.

23 What is the extent of your previous work
   experience (excluding sandwich placements)?
   _____ months

NON-SANDWICH GRADUATES

24 What is the extent of your previous work
   experience (including vacation work)?
   _____ months

25 How much of your previous work experience is:
   a) with the company you are joining? ___ months

   b) related to the work you are entering
      (but not with the company you are joining)?
      _____ months

26 How many jobs did you apply for in a formal
    way? _____

27 How many job offers did you receive? _____

28 According to your original personal preference,
    where does the job you have accepted rank among
    the total number you applied for (first, second
    etc.)? _____

29 How important were the following factors in your
    decision to accept the job? (If you are a
    sponsored sandwich graduate, indicate which
    factors were important to you in accepting the
    original offer of sponsorship). Please circle the
    appropriate number.

```
        5         4        3        2        1
A very important      Somewhat          Not very
consideration         important         important
```

    a) The advice of others   5   4   3   2   1

    b) The desire/need to be   5   4   3   2   1
       in a specific location

    c) Interest in the job   5   4   3   2   1
       itself

    d) The constraints of the   5   4   3   2   1
       graduate labour market
       at this time

    e) Remuneration   5   4   3   2   1

30 If you had to find a new job within a year, how
    easy would it be for you to move, compared to
    other graduates in your field? Please circle
    the appropriate number

```
much easier                              much more
for me                                   difficult
    5        4        3        2        1  for me
                  about the
                    same
```

31 To what extent do you feel that you were influenced
    by others (e.g. family, friends etc.) in your choice
    of job?

```
decision made                                    decision
completely free                                  largely
from the influence                               influenced
of others                  5    4    3    2    1  by others
```

32 Different people tend to want different things from
    their job. Please rank each of the items below from
    one to ten in order of their importance to you.

    e.g., If "job security" is the most important aspect
    of your job, put figure "1" beside the item. If
    "good salary" is the next most important aspect,
    put figure "2" beside this item; and so on until
    all 10 items are ranked.

    a) Varied work   ____

    b) Opportunity to use abilities   ____

    c) Good salary   ____

    d) Intellectual challenge   ____

    e) Opportunities for promotion   ____

    f) Good working conditions   ____

    g) Opportunity to manage   ____

    h) Job security   ____

    i) High amount of responsibility   ____

    j) Friendly colleagues   ____

33 How much do you feel you know about the company
    you are joining?

```
A great                        Very
deal                           little
          5    4    3    2    1
```

34 In your opinion, how accurate is the information
    you have about the company?

```
Very                           Very
accurate                       inaccurate
          5    4    3    2    1
```

35 What were your main sources of information about the company? (Rank 1, 2 ... as far as appropriate, according to amount of information)

a) careers service _____

b) company brochures _____

c) academic staff _____

d) interviews _____

e) company visits _____

f) family/friends _____

g) other (specify) _____ _____

36 The what extent do you feel it will be easy to change jobs within the next year should you decide to do so?

very difficult   very easy
for me to move   for me to
              5   4   3   2   1 move

37 If you were at all active in extra-curricular affairs, how would you rank your activities in terms of their relative importance on your development? (Please write the number 1 beside the most influential, and continue on with 2, 3 etc. as far as appropriate).

Type of activity	Example	Ranking
a) Sport	tennis, football	_____
b) Social	concerts, disco	_____
c) Arts	music, drama	_____
d) Politics	student's union	_____
e) Religious	bible-study	_____
f) Community	local social work	_____
g) other (please describe)		_____

38 Which political party would you support in the
next election?

   1. Conservative   4. S.D.P.
   2. Labour   5. Other (Please describe)
   3. Liberal

39 Please describe your religious conviction or
affiliation, if any?

   1. atheist   4. nominal Christian
   2. agnostic   5. other (please describe)
   3. active Christian _____

40 To what extent to you feel your life is influenced
by your convictions or affiliations mentioned above?

   very much   not at all
               5   4   3   2   1

41 How long do you plan to remain with the company
you are joining? Please circle the appropriate
number.

   1. less than 1 year   4. 3 - 4 years
   2. 1 -2 years   5. 4 - 5 years
   3. 2 - 3 years   6. 5 - 10 years
                          7. over 10 years

Thank you for your help. It is much appreciated. Once again,
let me emphasise that your replies will be treated with utmost
confidentiality.

When you have completed everything please return it to me
promptly using the enclosed stamped, addressed envelope.

GRADUATES AND WORK (2)

Like the first questionnaire, this one is strictly
confidential and the researcher guarantees that the identity
of the respondent will not be disclosed to the employer at any
time.

Again, it would be helpful if you could answer all questions
as honestly as possible. Where alternatives are given please
circle (e.g. 2) the appropriate number.

CODE

1 Name _____ Date _____

2 Company Name _____

3 Division and address of Company _____

   _____

4 Present salary (per annum)

   (1) up to £4999   (3) £6000 to £6999   (5) £8000 or
                                                  more
   (2) £5000 to £5999   (4) £7000 to £7999

5 How many full months have you been working for this
   company since graduating? _____

6 Please indicate how you feel about each aspect of your
   present job/placement listed below by circling the
   appropriate number.

5	4	3	2	1
Very satisfied	Satisfied	Neutral	Dissatisfied	Very Dissatisfied

   a) The personal relationships I have   5   4   3   2   1
      with my colleagues

   b) The amount of job security I have   5   4   3   2   1

   c) The chance to manage others   5   4   3   2   1

166

d) The amount of responsibility   5   4   3   2   1
   I have

e) My working conditions   5   4   3   2   1

f) The intellectual challenge my job 5   4   3   2   1
   gives me

g) The amount of salary I receive   5   4   3   2   1

h) The opportunities for promotion   5   4   3   2   1

i) The extent to which my job uses my 5   4   3   2   1
   abilities

j) The level of variety present in my 5   4   3   2   1
   job

In the following section if you are still on a training
programme, or yet to be placed, please answer questions
(7) - (10) OR questions (11) - (13) if you have already
been placed in a permanent job

NOT YET PLACED

7   What is your title at present? (e.g. Graduate Trainee)

   _____

8   What functional department? (e.g. Design Engineering,
    Systems, etc.) _____

9   When will your training finish? (month and year)

   _____

10 How sure are you of being offered a placement of your
    choice at the completion of your training? Please
    circle the appropriate number.

            5   4   3   2   1
    Certain   Very unsure

PLACED

11 What is you job title at present? _____

12 Which functional? department (e.g. Design Engineering, Systems etc.) _____

13 How would you describe your job placement with reference to your original choice? Please circle the appropriate number.

| Exactly what I want | 5 | 4 | 3 | 2 | 1 | Not what I wanted at all |

14 On the basis of what you already know about the job and organization you have joined, how accurate are the following statements? Please circle the appropriate number.

| 4 | 3 | 2 | 1 | 0 |

A very accurate description   A very inaccurate description   Do now know at stage

a) There are good career prospects in this company   4 3 2 1 0

b) Graduate entrants receive individual training   4 3 2 1 0

c) Company policies are fair   4 3 2 1 0

d) Movement from one department/ location to another is fairly easy   4 3 2 1 0

e) There is a relaxed, friendly atmosphere in the department   4 3 2 1 0

f) The well-being of people is of prime importance to management   4 3 2 1 0

g) The job involves a wide range of different activities   4 3 2 1 0

h) Compared to other companies the salary is good   4 3 2 1 0

i) Working hours are flexible   4 3 2 1 0

j) The company offers steady employment for the foreseeable future   4 3 2 1 0

168

k) The working conditions are good   4   3   2   1   0

l) The job makes use of individual   4   3   2   1   0
    abilities

m) There is opportunity for travel in   4   3   2   1   0
    the job

n) The job provides a sense of   4   3   2   1   0
    intellectual acheivement

o) The work is interesting   4   3   2   1   0

p) The job gives a high amount   4   3   2   1   0
   ·responsibility

q) The job involves being in charge   4   3   2   1   0
    of other people

r) Further professional training and   4   3   2   1   0
    education is encouraged

s) The job entails working under   4   3   2   1   0
    pressure

t) The recreational facilities   4   3   2   1   0
    provided by the company are of a
    high standard

15   To what extent do you see work friends outside work?

            5   4   3   2   1
      Regularly   Not at all

16   What have you received in the way of feedback on your
    work performance so far?   Please circle one
    alternative.

     1. Written performance   4. Occasional
       appraisal   informal feedback

     2. Verbal performance   5. No feedback at all
       appraisal

     3. Regular informal feedback

17   How would you rate the induction/training you have

received from the company so far? Please circle
the appropriate number.

                     5   4   3   2   1
         Excellent   Poor

18 Listed below are a series of statements that represent
    possible feelings that individuals might have about the
    organization for which they have chosen to work.
    Please think about the organization for which you are
    working and indicate the degree of your agreement or
    disagreement with each statement by circling one of the
    5 alternatives next to each statement.

                     5   4   3   2   1

         Strongly   Neither   Strongly
         agree   disagree   disagree
                         nor agree

    a) I am willing to put in a great deal   5 4 3 2 1
       of effort beyond that normally
       expected, in order to help this
       organization be successful

    b) I talk favourably about this   5 4 3 2 1
       organization with my friends
       as a great organization to work
       for

    c) I feel very little loyalty to this   5 4 3 2 1
       organization

    d) I would accept almost any type of   5 4 3 2 1
       job assignment to continue working
       with this organization

    e) I find that my values and this   5 4 3 2 1
       organization's values are very
       similar

    f) I am proud to tell others that I am   5 4 3 2 1
       part of this organization

    g) I could just as well be working   5 4 3 2 1
       for another organization so long
       as the job is similar

    h) I believe this organization will   5 4 3 2 1

really inspire the very best in me
in the way of job performance

i) It would take very little change in   5   4   3   2   1
my present circumstances to cause me
to want to leave the organization

j) I am extremely glad that I chose this 5   4   3   2   1
organization to work in over other
organizations I considered joining

k) There's not much to be gained by   5   4   3   2   1
sticking with this organization
indefinitely

l) I expect to often find it difficult   5   4   3   2   1
to agree with the organisation's rules
and regulations on matters relating
to employees

m) I really care about the fate of this   5   4   3   2   1
organization

n) For me, this organization is the best 5   4   3   2   1
of all my possible opportunities

o) Deciding to join this organization   5   4   3   2   1
was a definite mistake on my part

19   Different people tend to want different things from
their job. Please rank each of the items below from
one to ten in order of their importance to you.

E.g., if 'job security' is the most important part of
your job, put figure '1' beside that item. If 'good
salary' is the next most important aspect, put figure
'2' beside this item; and so on until all 10 items
are ranked. (Please avoid giving 2 or more items the
same rank.)

a) Varied work   _____

b) Opportunity to use
abilities   _____

c) Good salary   _____

d) Intellectual challenge   _____

e) Opportunities for
   promotions   _____

f) Good working conditions _____

g) Opportunity to manage
   others   _____

h) Job security   _____

i) High amount of
   reponsibility   _____

j) Friendly colleagues _____

20 Overall, how satisfied are you with your job?
    Please circle the appropriate number.

    Very   5   4   3   2   1   Very
    satisfied   dissatisfied

21 To what extent would you prefer another more ideal job
    (perhaps one not offered) other than the one you
    accepted?

    I would strongly   5 4 3 2 1   No desire for
    prefer another   another job other
    job   than the one I
                                       accepted

22 If you had your own way, will you be working for this
    organization in 3 years from now? Please circle the
    appropriate number.

    1. Certainly   3. Not sure   5. Certainly not
    2. Probably   4. Probably not

23 To what extent do you feel it will be easy to change
    jobs within the next year, should you decide to do so?

    very difficult   5 4 3 2 1   Very easy for me
    for me to move   to move

24 How long do you plan to remain with this organization?

1. Less than one year   4. 3-4 years
2. 1-2 years   5. 4-5 years
3. 2-3 years   6. 5-10 years
                               7. Over 10 years

25 Are you working with the same company you joined after
   graduating? If no, what was the main reason for leaving?

   _____

   _____

   _____

   _____

26 Since beginning work, have there been any major
   unanticipated surprises for you in your job? (If yes,
   please describe) _____

   _____

   _____

   _____

27 Thinking back over your experience of the last few months
   as a graduate settling into industry, what are some of the
   most significant events (good and/or bad) that you recall that
   helped or hindered that transition?

Event (situation, person)   Reason for significance

   _____   _____

   _____   _____

   _____   _____

28 In your opinion, what - if anything - could be done to
   improve the integration of graduates into industry?

   _____

   _____

   _____

Bibliography

Alderfer C P (1972) <u>Human Needs in Organizational Settings</u> Free Press of Glenco, New York.

Angle H L & Perry J L (1979) An Empirical Assessment ofOrganizational Commitment and Organizational Effectiveness <u>Administrative Science Quarterly</u> Mar 1981 Vol 26, (pps1-14)

ASET (1981) Association for Sandwich Education and Training, 1981 Journal.

Atton R (1982) <u>Seven Years After</u> MSc Dissertation Brunel University.

Berger P L and Luckman T (1967) <u>The Social Construction of reality: A Treatise in the Sociology of Knowledge</u> New York: Doubleday.

Blau P M, Gustad J W, Jesson R,Parnes H S, Wilcox,R C(1968) Occupational Choice A Conceptual Framework. <u>Industrial and Labour Relations Review</u>, Vol 9 No 4. pp.531, 536-7, 543.

Bray D W, Campbell R J, Grant D L,(1974) <u>Formative Years in Business</u>. Wiley, New York.

Brehm J W and Cohen A R (1959) Reevaluation of choice alternatives as a function of their number and qualitative similarity. <u>Journal of Abnormal and Social Psychology</u> 52, pp.384-389.

Brehm J W (1956) Post-decision changes in the desirability of alternatives, <u>Journal of Abnormal and Social Psychology,</u> 52, pp.384-389.

British Institute of Management <u>The Employment of Graduates</u> (1968) Information Summary No. 132.

Brock T C (1963) Effects of prior dishonesty on post decision dissonance. <u>Journal of Abnormal and Social Psychology</u> 66 pps 325-331

Buchanan B (1974)Building Organizational Commitment: the socialisation of Managers in Work Organizations. <u>Administrative Science Quarterly</u>, Vol. 19 No.4. pps 533-546.
Comer R and Laird J D (1975) Choosing to suffer as a consequence of expecting to suffer: Why do people do it? <u>Journal of Personality and Social Psychology</u> 32,92-101

Crites J O (1969) <u>Vocational Psychology</u> New York: McGraw Hill 1969.

Daniel W W and Pugh H (1975) Sandwich Courses in Higher Education PEP Report on CNAA Degrees in Business Studies Vol XL1 Broadsheet No. 557.

Davis J A (1965) Undergraduate Career Decisions Chicago: Aldine Publishing Co.

Denbury, G (ed) (1976) National Conference on Degree Sandwich Courses Universities Committee on Integrated Sandwich Courses.

Dugoni B L and Ilgen D R (1981) Realistic Job Previews and the adjustment of New Employees. Academy of Management Journal 1981 Vol.24 No.3 pps 579-591 Dunette M D, Arvey R D, Banas P A (1973) Why do they leave?

Personnel May/June pps 25-39

Dunette M D (1966) Personnel Selection and Placement Belmont, Calif: Wadsworth.

Farr J L, O'Leary B S and Bartlett C J (1973) Effect of a work sample test upon self selection and turnover of job applicants. Journal of Applied Psychology, 58 pps 283-285.

Festinger L (1957) Theory of Cognitive Dissonance Evanston, Illinois: Row, Peterson.

Festinger L and and Carlsmith J M (1959) Cognitive consequences of forced compliance. Journal of Abnormal and Social Psychology 58 pps 203-210.

Finkelman J M and Glass D C (1970) Reappraisal of the relationship between noise and human performance by means of subsidiary test measure. Journal of Applied Psychology 54 pps 211-213.

Finniston Sir M (1980) Engineering our Future, Dept of Industry, HMSO, London.

Folger R, Rosenfield D, Hayes R, (1978) Equity and Intrinsic Motivation: The role of choice, Journal of Personality and Social Psychology Vol 36, pps 557-564

Frederico S, Frederico P and Lundquist G (1976) Predicting women's turnover as a function of extent of met salary expectations and bio-demographic data. Personnel Psychology, 29 pps 559-566

Gerard H B (1968) Basic Features of Commitment in Theories of

Cognitive Consistency: A Sourcebook. ed by R P Adelson, M E Aronson, W J McGuire, T Newcombe M Rosenberg, P Tannenbaum, Rand McNally and Co: Chicago.

Ginzberg E, Ginsberg S W, Axelrad S and Herman J L (1951) Occupational Choice: An Approach to a General Theory Columbia Uni. Press New York.

Gleeson D (1980) Streaming at work and college: on the social differentiation of craft and technical apprentices in technical ed. Sociological Review Vol. 28 No. 4.

Greenaway H and Williams G (1973)   Patterns of change in graduate employment, Society of research into Higher Education.

Greeley A W (1968) Influence of the Religious factor on career plans and occupational values of college graduates.   American Journal of Sociolgy, May Vol 68.

Hackman J R, Lawler E (1971) Employee Reactions to Job Characteristics, Journal of Applied Psychology Monograph, Vol 55, No. 3.

Hall D T, Schneider B and Nygren H T (1970) Personal Factors in organizational identification.   Administrative Science Quarterly, 15 pps 363-367.

Hardin E (1965) Perceived and actual change in job satisfaction, Journal of Applied Psychology, 49 pps 363-367.

Hayes J (1973) Occupational Perceptions and Occupational information, Institute of Careers Officers, Vocational Guidance Research Unit. (Leeds Univ).

Herriot P, Ecob R, Hutchinson M (1980) Decision Theory and occupational choice: some longitudinal data. Journal of Occupational Psychology 52, 311-24.

Hill C P (1969) A Survey of university graduates in Shell. Shell International Petroleum Company Ltd, London.

Hrebiniak L G and Alutto J A (1972) Personal and role-Related Factors in the development of organizational commitment. Administrative Science Quarterly, Vol. 17 No 4 pps 555-573.

Hutt R and Parsons D (1981) Getting the drift of graduate mobility, Personnel Management, March pp 29-31, 43.

Ilgen D R and Seely W (1974) Realistic expectations as an aid in reducing voluntary redundancy. Journal of Applied Psychology Vol 59, No. 4.

Jahoda M (1963) The Education of Technologists Tavistock (London)

Katzell M E (1968) Expectations and Dropouts in Schools of Nursing, Journal of Applied Psychology, Vol.52 No.2 pps 154-157.

Keil E T, Riddell D S, Youth and Work: problems and perspectives, Sociological Review 14 (2) pps 117-37.

Kelsall R K, Poole A Kuhn (1970) Six Years After, Sheffield Higher Education Research Unit; Uni of Sheffield.

Kelsall, R K, Poole A, Kuhn A Graduates: the Sociology of an Elite. London, Methuen and Co Ltd.

Kiesler C A (1971) The Psychology of Commitment Academic Press: New York of London

Kiesler C A and Sakamura J (1966) A clarification of the Concept Occupational Choice, Rural Sociology Vol. 31, No 3. pps 265-276.

Lawler E, Kuleck W J, Rhode J G, Sorenson J E (1975) Job choice and post-choice dissonance. Organizational Behaviour and Human Performance No. 13, pps 133-145.

Lenski G (1960) The Religious Factor, Garden City, New York: Doubleby and Co.

Lepper M R and Greene D (1975) Turning play into work: effects of adult surveillance and extrinsic motivation. Journal of Personality and Social Psychology Vol. 31 No. 3 pps 479-486.

Louis M R (1980) Surprise and sense-making: what newcomers experience in entering unfamiliar organizational settings. Administrative Science Quarterly June Vol 25 pps 226-251.

Mansfield R (1971) Career development in the First Year at Work. Occupational Psychology 45 pps 139-149.

Mansfield R (1970) Graduates - why they leave industry Further Education 1 spring

Mansfield R (1972) The initiation of Graduates in Industry, Human Relations, Vol 25 pps 77-86.

Mansfield R and Davies T (1971) Occupational Choice at Oxford Further Education 2, 60-3.

March J G and Simon H A (1958) Organizations New York: Wiley.

McFalls J A , Gallagher B J (1979) Political orientation and occupational values of college youth, Adolescence, Vol 14, (56)

Mobley W H, Hand H H, Meglino B M and Griffith R W (1979) Review and conceptual analysis of the employee turnover process Psychological Bulletin, Vol 85, pps 493-522.

Morse J J (1975) Person job congruence and individual adjustment, Human Relations 28, pps 841-861.

Mortimer J J and Lorence J (1979) Work Experience and Occupational Value Socialisation, American Journal of Sociology, Vol 84 No 6.

Mowday R T, Steers R M and Porter L W (1979) The measurement of organizational commitment. Journal of Vocational Behaviour 14 pps 224-247.

Muchinsky and Tuttle M L (1979) The measurement of organizational commitment, Journal of Vocational Behaviour, 14 pps 43-77.

Mynatt C and Sherman S J (1975) Responsibility attributing in groups and individuals: direct test of diffusion of responsibility hypothesis, Journal of Personality and Social Psychology, Vol 31, No 5 pps 1111-1118.

Oliver R L (1977) Effect of expectations and disconfirmation on postexposure product evaluations: an alternative interpretation. Journal of Applied Psychology. Vol 62, No 4 pps 480-486.

O'Brien G E, Dowling P (1980) The effects of congruency between perceived and desired job attributes upon job satisfaction. Journal of Applied Psychology. 53 pps 212-230.

O'Reilly C A and Caldwell D F (1980) Job Choice: The impact of intrinsic and extrinsic factors on subsequent satisfaction and commitment, Journal of Applied Psychology, 65 No 5 pp 559-565.

O'Reilly C A and Caldwell D F (1980) The commitment and job

tenure of new employees: some evidence of post decisional justification. Administrative Science Quarterly 26 pps 597-616.

Pallak M S, Sogin S R and Van Zante A (1974) Bad decisions: effects of volition locus of causality, and negative consequences on attitude change. Journal of Personality and Social Psychology 30 pps 217-227.

Parsons D and Hutt R (1981) The Mobility of Young Graduates Institute of Manpower Studies IMS Report No. 26, University Sussex.

Pearce D S and Jackson K F (1976) The Graduate Connection CRAC

Pearson R (1976) Qualified Managers in Employment Institute of Manpower Studies.

Political and Economic Planning (1956) Graduates in Industry George Allen and Unwin, London.

Pfeffer J and Lawler J (1980) Effects of Job Alternatives, Extrinsic Rewards and Behavioural Commitment on Attitude Toward the Organization. Administrative Science Quarterly, Mar Vol 25 pps 38-56.

Porter L W and Steers R M (1973) Organizational, Work and Personal Factors in Employee Turnover and Absenteeism. Psychological Bulletin, Vol 80, No 2 pps 151-176.

Porter L W, Steers R M, Mowday R T, Boulian P V (1974) Organizational Commitment, Job Satisfaction and Turnover among Psychiatric Technicians. Journal of Applied Psychology. Vol 59 No 5 pps 603-9.

Posner B Z (1981) Comparing recruiter, student and faculty perceptions of important applicant and job characteristics Personnel Psychology, 34 pps 329-339.

Price J L (1977) The Study of Turnover, The Iowa State Univ. Press: Iowa.

Reed J V, Duncan K and Vallance P J (Eds) (1980) Cooperative Education Today, Universities Committee for Integrated Sandwich Courses, 1980 NFER Publishing Co, Windsor, UK.

Reilly R R, Tenopyr M L and Sperling S M (1979), Effects of job previews on job acceptance and survival of telephone operator candidates, Journal of Applied Psychology 64 pps 218-220.

Roberts K (1968), The entry into employment Sociological Review, Vol 2, pps 264-273

Rogers T G P and Williams P (1970) The Recruitment and Training of Graduates IMP London

Rosenberg M (1957) Occupation and Values, Chicago: Free Press.

Ross I O and Zander A (1957) Need Satisfactions of Employee Turnover, Personnel Psychology Vol 10 pps 327-338.

Salancik G R (1977) Commitment and the control of organizational behaviour and belief in Staw B and Salancik G R (eds) New Directions in Organizational Behaviour, St Clair Press: Chicago.

Salancik G R and Pfeffer J (1977) An examination of the need satisfaction models of job attitudes Administrative Science Quarterly 22, pps 427-456.

Schein E H (1964) How to break in the college graduate Harvard Business Review, 42, pps 68-76

Schein E H (1978) Career Dynamics, Addison Wesley: Reading, Mass.

Schneider B (1975a) Organizational Climate - Individual Preferences and Organizational Realities Revisited, Journal of Applied Psychology, Vol 60, No 4 pps 459-65

Schneider B (1975b) Organizational Climates: an essay Personnel Psychology 28 pps 447-481.

Slocum W L (1967) Occupational Careers : A Sociological Perspective, Aldine: Chicago.

Snow T (1973) Observations on the present crisis in Patterns of Change in graduate employment. Greenaway and Williams (eds) SRHE

Sofer C (1970) Men Mid-Career Cambridge: University Press

Stanworth P and Giddens A (1974) An economic elite: a demographic profile of company chairman in Elite and Power in British Society, Stanworth and Giddens (eds) Cambridge University Press.

Staw B M (1980) Rationality and justification in Organizational life in Staw B M and Cummings L L (eds) Research in Organizational Behaviour JAI Press Inc: Greenwich, Connecticut

Staw B M and Fox F V (1977) Escalation: The determinants of Commitment to a chosen course of action. Human Relations Vol 30 No 5 pps 431-450.

Super D E (1953) A theory of vocational development American Psychologist, 8 pps 185-190.

Swinnerton-Dyer P (1982) Report of the working party in post-graduate education, to the Advisory Boards for the Research Councils. HMSO.

Timperley S (1974) Personnel Planning and Occupational Choice George Allen and Unwin Ltd, London.

Titma M (1979) Formation of Young People's Orientation towards Work Acta Sociologica, Vol 22 No 4.

Tom V R (1971) The Role of Personality of Organizational Images in the Recruiting Process. Organizational Behaviour and Human Performance 6pps 573-92.

Ullman J C and Gutteridge T C Job Search in the labour market for college graduates: A case study of MBAs, Academy of Management Journal, June 1974 Vol 17, No 2 pps 381-386.

Underhill R (1966) Values and post-college career change, American Journal of Sociology, Vol 72.

Van Maanen J (1976) Breaking in Socialisation to Work in R Dubin (ed) Handbook of Work, Organization and society Rand McNally College, Chicago.

Vroom V H and Deci D L (1971) The stability of post-decision dissonance. Organizational Behaviour and Human Performance 1 pps 212-225.

Vroom V H (1964) Work and Motivation New York: Wiley.

Wakeford F and J (1974) University and the study of elites in Elites and Power in British Society, Stanworth and Giddens (eds) Cambridge University Press.

Wanour (1975) A job preview makes recruiting more effective. Harvard Business Review 53 (5) pps 16, 166, 168.

Wanous J P (1976) Organizational Entry: from naive expectations to realistic beliefs Journal of Applied Psychology Vol 61 No 1 pps 22-29.

Wanous J P (1977) Organizational Entry: Newcomers moving from outside to inside Psychological Bulletin Vol 81 July pps 601-617.

Wanous J P (1978) Realistic Job Previews: Can a procedure to reduce turnover also influence the relationship between abilities and performance, Personnel Psychology, Vol 31 (2) pps 249-258.

Wanous J P (1980) Organizational Entry Addison Wesley: Reading MA

Ward L B and Athos A G (1972) Student Expectations of Corporate Life: Implications for Management Recruiting. Boston, Division of Research, Harvard Uni.

Weick K E (1969) The Social Psychology of Organising Reading, Mass: Addison - Wesley.

Weitz J (1956) Job Expectancy and Survival, Journal of Applied Psychology, 40 pps 245-247.

White S (1968) The process of Occupational Choice British Journal of Industrial Relations Vol 6 No 2 pps 168-84.

Williamson P (1981) Early Careers of 1970 Graduates Unit for Manpower Studies Research Paper No 26 Dept of Employment.

Williamson P (1979) Moving around the room at the top Dept of Employment Gazette pps 1120-1228.

Windolf P (1982) Recruitment and selection in enterprises International Institute of Management/labour Market Policy 82-17 Berlin.

Youngberg C F (1963) An experimental study of job satisfaction and turnover in relation to job expectations and self expectations unpublished doctoral dissertation New York University.